*Dear Ray,*

*God bless you,*

# Go in Peace

YOUR GUIDE TO THE PURPOSE AND POWER OF CONFESSION

**Father Mitch Pacwa, S.J., Ph.D.**
**and Sean Brown, M.A.**

*Fr. Mitch Pacwa, SJ*

# ASCENSION PRESS

West Chester, Pennsylvania

Ascension Press
Post Office Box 1990
West Chester, PA 19380
Orders: 1-800-376-0520
www.AscensionPress.com

Cover design: The Design Works Group, Inc., Sisters, Oregon

Printed in the United States of America
09 10 11 12 9 8 7 6 5 4 3

ISBN-13: 978-1-932927-95-5

*To Our Lady, the Mother of Mercy*
*and Refuge of Sinners*

# Contents

# *Acknowledgments*

M any thanks to Matthew Pinto and the entire team at
Ascension for making this book a reality; to Michael
J. Miller for his editing of the questions and answers and
his many helpful suggestions; to the Design Works Group
for their creative cover design; and to all priests who
reconcile souls to God through this wonderful sacrament
of God's grace.

# Key to Biblical Abbreviations

The following abbreviations are used for the various Scriptural verses cited throughout the book. (Note: CCC = *Catechism of the Catholic Church*.)

*Old Testament*

| | | | |
|---|---|---|---|
| Gn | Genesis | Jon | Jonah |
| Ex | Exodus | Mi | Micah |
| Lv | Leviticus | Na | Nahum |
| Nm | Numbers | Hb | Habakkuk |
| Dt | Deuteronomy | Zep | Zephaniah |
| Jos | Joshua | Hg | Haggai |
| Jgs | Judges | Zec | Zechariah |
| Ru | Ruth | Mal | Malachi |
| 1 Sam | 1 Samuel | | |
| 2 Sam | 2 Samuel | | *New Testament* |
| 1 Kgs | 1 Kings | M t | Matthew |
| 2 Kgs | 2 Kings | Mk | Mark |
| 1 Chr | 1 Chronicles 2 | Lk | Luke |
| Chr | 2 Chronicles | Jn | John |
| Ezr | Ezra | Acts | Acts |
| Neh | Nehemiah | Rom | Romans |
| Tb | Tobit | 1 Cor | 1 Corinthians |
| Jdt | Judith | 2 Cor | 2 Corinthians |
| Est | Esther | Gal | Galatians |
| 1 Mc | 1 Maccabees | Eph | Ephesians |
| 2 Mc | 2 Maccabees | Phil | Philippians |
| Jb | Job | Col | Colossians |
| Ps | Psalms | 1 Thess | 1 Thessalonians |
| Prv | Proverbs | 2 Thess | 2 Thessalonians |
| Eccl | Ecclesiastes | 1 Tm | 1 Timothy |
| Sng | Song of Songs | 2 Tm | 2 Timothy |
| Wis | Wisdom | Ti | Titus |
| Sir | Sirach | Phlm | Philemon |
| Is | Isaiah | Heb | Hebrews |
| Jer | Jeremiah | Jas | James |
| Lam | Lamentations | 1 Pt | 1 Peter |
| Bar | Baruch | 2 Pt | 2 Peter |
| Ez | Ezekiel | 1 Jn | 1 John |
| Dn | Daniel | 2 Jn | 2 John |
| Hos | Hosea | 3 Jn | 3 John |
| Jl | Joel | Jude | Jude |
| Am | Amos | Rv | Revelation |
| Ob | Obadiah | | |

# 101 Questions and Answers

## 1. What is confession?

"Confession" is the name popularly given to the sacrament of the Catholic Church by which sins committed after baptism are forgiven. However, confession is just one element of this sacrament. Its other necessary elements include penance, reconciliation, and absolution, all of which will be discussed in later questions.

A *sacrament* is an outward sign instituted by Jesus Christ to communicate God's grace (CCC 1210). Christ gave the seven sacraments to the apostles, who celebrated them from the earliest days of the Church. It is the responsibility of the apostles' successors, the bishops, to ensure that the sacraments are celebrated in accord with the will of Christ.

"Confession" is the element of the sacrament of reconciliation in which a person acknowledges his or her personal sins and tells them to a priest. After listening to the confession, the priest may counsel the penitent; he will always impose a "penance"—that is, some prayer or an act of self-sacrifice or discipline designed to help heal the effects of sin in the penitent and to strengthen his or her commitment to sin no more. Finally, the priest, by virtue of his ordination and a *faculty* (i.e., delegated authority) given to him by the bishop, proclaims the words of absolution—"I absolve you from your sins, in the name of the Father, and of the Son, and of the Holy Spirit"—to declare that the person's sins are forgiven and that he or she is reconciled with God and His Church.

2. **I've also heard confession called "reconciliation" and "penance." Is there any difference between these terms?**

Each of these three terms—confession, penance, and reconciliation—describes one particular aspect of the very rich experience of receiving this sacrament. *Confession* emphasizes the act of accusing oneself of one's sins in the presence of Christ (represented by a priest, who is traditionally called a *confessor*). The term *penance* emphasizes the two aspects of personal repentance in this sacrament: first, conversion or turning away from sin, and second, the expression of sorrow through prayer, restitution, and sacrifice. (The person going to confession is commonly referred to as the *penitent*.) Finally, *reconciliation* describes the interpersonal effect of the sacrament, by which the penitent is reconciled with God and the Church.

On December 2, 1973, the Congregation for Divine Worship, the Vatican office which regulates the celebration of the sacraments, published a decree on confession which begins with and emphasizes reconciliation. Though the sacramental liturgy is officially called the "Rite of Penance," the term "reconciliation" emphasizes what God does for the penitent in the sacrament, rather than what the penitent does by confessing and performing acts of penance.

**3.  Is confession just a "Catholic thing" or do other Christians have this practice also?**

Some other Christian communities also celebrate the sacrament of reconciliation or confession. The Eastern Orthodox Churches, which have preserved apostolic succession through their bishops and therefore have a valid priesthood, include this sacrament among their seven. These Churches use the term "mystery" (from the Greek word *mysterion*) rather than sacrament, a Latin word meaning "oath" or "binding obligation," which came to mean "religious mystery" as well.

Most Protestant denominations do not recognize confession or reconciliation as one of their sacraments. Usually these are limited to baptism and holy communion, although some denominations also recognize confirmation, while others include marriage and ordination to the ministry among their sacraments. Some denominations do not believe in sacraments at all but prefer to speak of *ordinances*—that is, certain rituals which Christ ordained and commanded Christians to perform.

Nonetheless, most Protestant denominations recognize the need to confess one's sins. Therefore, some have instituted opportunities to meet in "the pastor's parlor" to confess sins and ask for prayer. Other denominations emphasize the communal confession of sin, particularly at revival meetings. In these experiences, though, the emphasis is on the penitent's act of faith in the power of Jesus to forgive sins rather than on any power or authority of the minister. Therefore, Protestant ministers do not pronounce any words of absolution.

## 4. Do any non-Christian religions have a practice similar to confession?

Yes, some non-Christian religions do have practices which are similar to confession. This fact illustrates the human need to confess one's moral failures to another person, not only for psychological reasons but also because of a deeper spiritual need to reconcile the reality of one's good, holy, and spiritual intentions with the reality of one's sins.

In Judaism, the High Holy Days include *Yom Kippur*, the "Day of Atonement," when the focus is on seeking God's pardon for the sins one has committed during the previous year (see Lv 23:27–28). This is a day for performing acts of penance, such as fasting for the entire day, in addition to participating in prayer at the synagogue. An expression of the power of this day is the popular belief that God opens His book and grants pardon for the sins that are confessed until the next time the book is opened during the following year's High Holy Days. In addition, individuals can "make *viddui*," confessing their sins to the rabbi as an expression of repentance and sorrow. However, the rabbi has no authority to offer forgiveness, since it is a key belief in rabbinic Judaism that only God can forgive sins.

## 5.   Isn't confession just an invention of the Church?

No. Confession, like all the seven sacraments of the Church, was instituted by Jesus Christ (CCC 1210). We can see this clearly in John 20:21–23, when Jesus appeared to His apostles on Easter Sunday night:

> Jesus said to them again, "Peace be with you. As the Father has sent me, even so I send you." And when he had said this, he breathed on them, and said to them, "Receive the Holy Spirit. If you forgive the sins of any, they are forgiven; if you retain the sins of any, they are retained."

This passage contains three key points: first, the power to forgive or retain sins is something entrusted to the apostles through the gift of the Holy Spirit, given from the Father through Jesus Christ; second, an audible confession is necessary so that the apostles and their successors can determine whether they should forgive or retain the particular sins confessed; and third, the apostles and their successors forgive or retain sins by the power of the Holy Spirit, and this forgiveness or retention is valid in heaven as well as on earth.

## 6.   Where else in the Bible is there evidence for the sacrament of confession?

In addition to the passage quoted in the previous answer, which recounts the institution of the sacrament, confession is described in several New Testament letters. James 5:14-16 exhorts Christians to administer two of the sacraments: the anointing of the sick and confession.

> Is any among you sick? Let him call for the elders of
> the church, and let them pray over him, anointing him
> with oil in the name of the Lord; and the prayer of faith
> will save the sick man, and the Lord will raise him
> up; and if he has committed sins, he will be forgiven.
> Therefore confess your sins to one another, and pray
> for one another, that you may be healed. The prayer of a
> righteous man has great power in its effects.

The term "elders" in 5:14 translates the Greek word *presbuteroi,* from which the German word *Priester* and the English word *priest* are derived. This passage, then, makes clear that the priest is the minister of the anointing of the sick. It is somewhat ambiguous regarding confession, in that it calls for the confession of sins "to one another." If one were to look to the Bible alone, this could be interpreted to mean any Christian, any "righteous man." However, since the Bible teaches us to "hold to the traditions which you were taught by us, either by word of mouth or by letter" (2 Thess 2:15), we can interpret this text as a reference to the Church's sacramental tradition of confessing one's sins to "presbyters" or priests.

St. Paul emphasizes the importance of the ministry of reconciliation in 2 Corinthians 5:17-20:

> Therefore, if any one is in Christ, he is a new creation;
> the old has passed away, behold, the new has come. All
> this is from God, who through Christ reconciled us
> to himself and gave us the ministry of reconciliation;
> that is, in Christ God was reconciling the world to
> himself, not counting their trespasses against them,
> and entrusting to us the message of reconciliation. So
> we are ambassadors for Christ, God making his appeal
> through us. We beseech you on behalf of Christ, be
> reconciled to God.

The key to this passage is that God has reconciled humanity to Himself through Jesus Christ by not counting their sins or trespasses against them (5:18-19). However, Christ has entrusted this message and ministry of reconciliation to St. Paul and other ministers, who see themselves as ambassadors of Christ. An ambassador acts on the authority of the king who sends him and can speak in the king's name and with his authority. Since the King—Jesus Christ—reconciles sinful humans to God, His ambassadors can authoritatively proclaim this same message. This passage provides a theological insight into John 20:22, where Christ the Risen Lord commissions the apostles to forgive sins.

Another passage that presents the apostles (and their successors) as stewards of God's mysteries is 1 Corinthians 4:1-2: "This is how one should regard us, as servants of Christ and stewards of the mysteries of God. Moreover it is required of stewards that they be found trustworthy." As we pointed out in the answer to question three, sacraments are also referred to as "mysteries" (*mysteria*), the same Greek term used by St. Paul in 4:1. So the apostles and their successors are the stewards of God's mysteries—not only in proclaiming the Gospel, which transcends human understanding, but also in administering the sacraments. One should note that both baptism and the Eucharist are important themes in this very epistle (see 1 Cor 6:11-13, 10:16-17, 11:23-30).

Thus, we can see clear evidence for the sacrament of confession in the Bible, both in the command that

Christ gave His apostles (see Jn 20:22) and in the teachings of the apostles James and Paul.

### 7.   What is necessary for a good sacramental confession?

A "good" confession (i.e., one that is pleasing to God and efficacious) has six main components:

1) *Examination of conscience.* The penitent needs to become aware that the actions he or she has committed are sins. He or she must then take personal responsibility for these sins and be sorry for having committed them. To truly repent of one's sins requires an actual grace from God.

2) *Firm purpose of amendment.* The penitent must make a resolution not to commit those particular sins again, with the help of God's grace.

3) *Confession.* The penitent confesses his or her sins in the sacrament of reconciliation.

4) *Penance.* The priest imposes a penance that the penitent must be able and willing to do.

5) *Contrition.* The penitent expresses sorrow for his or her sins and demonstrates a desire for reconciliation with God by praying an act of contrition.

6) *Absolution.* The priest pronounces the words of absolution and dismisses the penitent with the words "The Lord has freed you from your sins, go in peace."

## 8.  What is sin?

Sin is the deliberate and free decision to disobey God, who is all good, and to choose what is evil. The *Catechism of the Catholic Church* notes the undeniable presence of sin in human history and in our world today (CCC 386). The pervasiveness of sin is part of the human condition because of "original sin," the sin of our first parents, Adam and Eve. "Man, tempted by the devil, let his trust in his Creator die in his heart and, abusing his freedom, disobeyed God's command" (CCC 397). The evil of sin consists of "humanity's rejection of God and opposition to [Him]" (CCC 386). By committing sin, man prefers himself to God and thereby scorns his Creator, choosing "himself over and against God, against the requirements of his creaturely status and therefore against his own good" (CCC 398).

Although original sin is the reason why sin and death entered into the world that God created to be good, the responsibility for sin in human history does not lie with Adam and Eve alone. Because of our weakened human nature, every human being in every age—except Jesus Christ and His Mother Mary—is also guilty of actual sins, sins personally committed. Divine Revelation teaches about sin with more clarity than mere human philosophical reflection can attain. Some people are "tempted to explain [sin] as merely a developmental flaw, a psychological weakness, a mistake, or the necessary consequence of an inadequate social structure, etc. Only in the knowledge of God's plan for man can we grasp that sin is an abuse of the freedom that God gives to created persons so that they are capable of loving [Him] and loving one another" (CCC 387). Furthermore, divine revelation clarifies the consequences of forsaking God for a life of sin: eternal separation from God in hell (see Mt 5:22, 7:21-23; 1 Cor 6:9-10; Gal 5:19-21; 2 Thess 1:9; CCC 1035).

**9.  Are all actual sins equally serious?**

No, actual sins are serious to differing degrees. The Church recognizes two principal degrees of seriousness (or *gravity*) of sin: mortal and venial (see CCC 1854–1864). We can see this distinction in 1 John 5:16-17:

> If any one sees his brother committing what is not a mortal sin, he will ask, and God will give him life for those whose sin is not mortal. There is sin which is mortal; I do not say that one is to pray for that. All wrongdoing is sin, but there is sin which is not mortal.

This distinction in the gravity of moral evil is corroborated by human experience. For example, everyone recognizes that murder is a more serious crime than a fist fight.

Mortal sin, as a grave violation of the divine law, results in the complete loss of charity and of sanctifying grace (i.e., the "state of grace"), which is necessary for salvation. If a person in a state of mortal sin remains unrepentant until death, he or she will be eternally separated from God in hell (CCC 1861).

No one can commit a mortal sin by accident. For a sin to be mortal, three conditions must be fulfilled: 1) the sin must be objectively serious (or grave); 2) the person committing the sin must know that it is a grave matter; and 3) the person must freely choose to commit the offense. Note, however, that "feigned ignorance and hardness of heart (see Mk 3:5-6; Lk 16:19-31) do not diminish, but rather increase, the voluntary character of a sin" (CCC 1859). How do we know whether or not something is grave matter? The *Catechism* explains that grave matter is "specified by the Ten Commandments" and that "the gravity of sins is more or less great: murder is graver than theft. One must also take into account who is wronged: violence against parents is in itself graver than violence against a stranger" (CCC 1858).

The person who is unintentionally ignorant of moral laws and principles is certainly not considered as guilty of a grave offense as a knowledgeable person would be. Many people today, under the influence of our culture's lax moral sensibility, no longer consider having sexual relations outside of marriage or missing Mass on Sunday as serious matters. Therefore, their lack of awareness of the seriousness of these sins may mitigate—or even remove—their guilt.

In addition to ignorance, psychological and emotional disorders, as well as external pressures, can also mitigate one's moral culpability; some psychopathologies may even render one incapable of making a truly free choice. Such a person would not be able, then, to commit a mortal sin. Since the moral law is written on the human heart, though, no one can claim ignorance of its fundamental principles (see CCC 1860).

A venial sin is a less serious matter, yet it still is an action, thought, or omission that falls short of the standard required by the moral law. Furthermore, if someone "disobeys the moral law in a grave matter, but without full knowledge or without complete consent," this would be considered venially sinful (CCC 1862).

Though venial sin is not as serious as mortal sin, it has a number of negative effects. Every venial sin weakens charity—that is, it can make us less capable of choosing to love someone else because we prefer something sinful. An attachment to venial sin shows that we love certain things more than we love God. Venial sin hampers our growth in virtue by focusing our attention on satisfying our own desires rather than on the God's will for us. Deliberate venial sins, if we do not repent of them, dispose us little by little to commit mortal sin. By "allowing" ourselves to commit small infractions, we easily become prone to committing larger ones.

Even though "venial sin does not set us in direct opposition to the will and friendship of God... or break the covenant with God," its negative effects "merit temporal punishment" either in this life or in purgatory (see CCC 1863; also, questions 83–87 on purgatory).

**10. Can a single mortal sin really be enough to cause someone to be condemned to hell?**

Yes. Just as one wrong turn on a road trip is sufficient to prevent a person from reaching his or her destination, so too one mortal sin can prevent a soul from reaching heaven. Union with God in the joys of heaven requires that a person freely chooses to love

Him. However, freely choosing to commit a serious sin redirects the human heart from the love of God, which is both the *means* of getting to heaven as well as the *purpose* of being in heaven. In effect, the sinner's soul freely separates itself from God's love—preferring creation over the Creator—and this decision is enough to exclude that soul from heaven for all eternity (CCC 1033).

The Bible teaches these truths in a number of places. The first epistle of John warns that hatred ultimately leads to eternal condemnation: "He who does not love remains in death. Anyone who hates his brother is a murderer, and you know that no murderer has eternal life abiding in him" (1 Jn 3:14–15). In the Sermon on the Mount, Jesus warns that a number of sins can place one in jeopardy of hell:

> But I say to you that every one who is angry with his brother shall be liable to judgment; whoever insults his brother shall be liable to the council, and whoever says, "You fool!"' shall be liable to the hell of fire ... You have heard that it was said, "You shall not commit adultery." But I say to you that every one who looks at a woman lustfully has already committed adultery with her in his heart. If your right eye causes you to sin, pluck it out and throw it away; it is better that you lose one of your members than that your whole body be thrown into hell (Mt 5:22, 27–29).

Jesus also warns us that we shall be separated from Him if we fail to meet the serious needs of the poor and the little ones who are His brethren (see Mt 25:31-46).

## 11. Do the Bible and the Church really teach that God condemns people to hell?

Yes. Both the Bible and the constant teaching of the Church affirm both the existence of hell and the fact that those who persist in their sins and reject God's grace will be condemned to spend eternity there (see CCC 1033–1037). As the *Catechism* puts it, "to die in mortal sin without repenting and accepting God's merciful love means remaining separated from him forever *by our own free choice*" (CCC 1033, emphasis added). So, while we can speak of "God condemning people to hell," in actuality, those who end up in hell have condemned themselves by choosing to remain in their sins.

In Matthew 22:1-14, Jesus tells a parable about God's invitation to His wedding feast (i.e., heaven). In this parable, the king (representing God the Father) says to a guest who entered without a wedding garment, "'Friend, how did you get in here without a wedding garment?' And he was speechless. Then the king said to the attendants, 'Bind him hand and foot, and cast him into the outer darkness; there men will weep and gnash their teeth.' For many are called, but few are chosen" (Mt 22:12-13).

This parable clearly teaches the reality of judgment, condemnation, and hell, and that those who are found without the "wedding garment" of God's grace will be excluded from the feast. In the Chapter 25 of Matthew's gospel, Jesus discusses the kingdom of heaven and presents several parables which describe a similar judgment: the parable of the foolish maidens who had not prepared enough oil for themselves (Mt 25:1-13), the parable of the servant who hid the "talent" (i.e., money) his master had entrusted him with instead of investing and increasing it (Mt 25:14-30), and the parable of the sheep and the goats (Mt 25:31-46).

The Church has consistently taught that those who freely choose to remain in the state of mortal sin will be condemned to an eternity separated from God. As the Dogmatic Constitution on the Church (*Lumen Gentium*) from the Second Vatican Council (1962–1965) affirms:

> Before we reign with Christ in glory we must all appear "before the judgment seat of Christ, so that each one may receive good or evil, according to what he has done in the body" (2 Cor 5:10), and at the end of the world "they will come forth, those who have done good, to the resurrection of life, and those who have done evil, to the resurrection of judgment" (Jn 5:29; see Mt 25:46). (*Lumen Gentium*, 48)

God predestines no one to hell, because each person has free will. This has been affirmed through the centuries by the Second Council of Orange (529) and the Council of Trent (1547). To be condemned, a person must willfully turn away from God by committing a mortal sin and persist in that state until the end of his or her life (CCC 1037). Until death, every person has an opportunity to repent of sin, turn to God, and seek His mercy.

The teaching of Scripture and the Church concerning the possibility of being condemned to hell is a call to take our eternal destiny seriously; it is an "urgent call to conversion" (CCC 1036). As Jesus warns in the Sermon on the Mount, "Enter by the narrow gate; for the gate is wide and the way is easy, that leads to destruction, and those who enter by it are many. For the gate is narrow and the way is hard, that leads to life, and those who find it are few" (Mt 7:13-14).

## 12. If Jesus died for our sins, why do we need to confess them?

First, let's be clear: The Church, as the steward and interpreter of Sacred Scripture, clearly affirms that Jesus Christ died for our sins (see CCC 601). As St. Paul states in his First Letter to the Corinthians, "Christ died for our sins in accordance with the [S]criptures" (1 Cor 15:3). Furthermore, the *Catechism* cites the Council of Quiercy, which taught in the year 853 that "There is not, never has been, and never will be a single human being for whom Christ did not suffer" (CCC 605). In addition, the Church's official instruction on how to celebrate the Rite of Penance teaches that Jesus Christ "died for our sins and rose for our justification," citing Romans 4:25.

When we go to confession, we are like Bob Dylan, "Knock, knock, knockin' on heaven's door." By dying for our sins, Jesus unlocked the door to forgiveness and to heaven. Without His saving death, we could plead and wail at the door forever, but we would remain shut out eternally in our own darkness, unable to open the door even a crack. However, the fact that Christ has opened the door does not mean that we have already walked through it to salvation. We must still do our part, going to the door by confessing our sins, asking Christ's pardon, and accepting the reconciliation He offers. Christ's own first proclamation was "the Kingdom of God is at hand; repent and believe in the gospel" (Mk 1:15). Each individual must approach Christ crucified and ask for forgiveness, not of sin in general, but of the sins he or she has personally committed through his or her own fault.

### 13. Why can't we just confess our sins directly to God?

Actually, we can. The Catholic Church certainly does not forbid us from confessing our sins directly to God in prayer and asking for his forgiveness. But the Church has always affirmed the necessity of following Christ's instructions and confessing one's sins to a priest (see Jn 20:22). In fact, the confession of mortal sins is absolutely necessary, since mortal sins involve serious matters and, by definition, result in the loss of sanctifying grace. There are no limits to God's mercy, but the sacrament of reconciliation is the one ordinary way to receive absolution and be restored to the state of grace. There is great spiritual benefit to confessing one's venial sins as well, though these can be forgiven outside of sacramental confession (e.g., during the penitential rite at Mass, through reception of the Eucharist, etc.).

## 14. The Bible says that only God can forgive sins, not man.

First, as you correctly state in your question, the Bible is unequivocal (as is the *Catechism*; see CCC 1441) in teaching that God is the One who forgives sins. Here are just a few of the Old Testament passages which make this abundantly clear:

- "If you, O Lord, would mark iniquities, Lord, who could stand? But there is forgiveness with you that you may be feared" (Ps 130:3-4).

- "I am he who blots out your transgressions for my own sake, and I will not remember your sins" (Is 43:25).

- "Who is a God like you, pardoning iniquity and passing over transgression for the remnant of his inheritance? He does not retain his anger for ever because he delights in steadfast love. He will again have compassion upon us, he will tread our iniquities under foot. You will cast all our sins into the depths of the sea" (Mi 7:18).

- "To the Lord our God belong mercy and forgiveness, because we have rebelled against him" (Dn 9:9).

Interestingly, the New Testament texts which explicitly state that only God can forgive sins place this teaching in the mouth of the Pharisees, as they accuse Jesus of blasphemy:

- "Why does this man speak thus? It is blasphemy! Who can forgive sins but God alone?" (Mk 2:7)

- "And the scribes and the Pharisees began to question, saying, 'Who is this that speaks blasphemies? Who can forgive sins but God only?'" (Lk 5:21)

- "Then those who were at table with him began to say among themselves, 'Who is this, who even forgives sins?'" (Lk 7:49)

Note that in each instance the Pharisees make this statement of faith as a principle to deny the ability and right of Jesus to forgive sins! Christians understand Christ's words as evidence that He was aware both of His ability to forgive sins and therefore of His divinity. After He won the ultimate authority to reconcile sinners to God by dying on the Cross and rising from the dead, Jesus proceeded to confer this authority to His apostles on Easter Sunday night (see Jn 20:22; CCC 1441-1445). If Jesus is God and, as such, has the authority to forgive sins, then He also has the authority to confer this power on His apostles and on their successors, the bishops.

## 15. What actually happens in confession?

Simply put, the Church teaches that Jesus Christ, through the ministry of His priests, forgives our sins. This may lead one to wonder, "What does forgiveness entail?" By forgiving our sins, Christ does not merely "cover them up," nor does He simply turn away His Father's gaze from them. Rather, in the sacrament of reconciliation, the sinner in the darkness of the confessional meets the full power of Christ's death during a dark afternoon on Calvary. Confession does not merely sweep sins under a carpet, nor is it simply the satisfaction of a psychological self-help mind game. Rather, in confession, sins are truly washed away by the blood of Jesus Christ, thoroughly cleansing the sinner's soul.

### 16. At what point during confession are sins forgiven?

The point at which one's sins are forgiven in the sacrament of reconciliation is the pronouncement of absolution by the priest. The formula of absolution used in the revised Rite of Penance (1973) is as follows:

> God the Father of mercies, through the death and resurrection of his Son, has reconciled the world to himself and sent the Holy Spirit among us for the forgiveness of sins; through the ministry of the Church may God give you pardon and peace, and I absolve you from your sins in the name of the Father, and of the Son, and of the Holy Spirit.

The penitent responds with an affirmation of faith in the gift of absolution by saying "Amen."

While absolution is the actual "moment" of forgiveness of sins, the entire celebration of this sacrament is a moment for receiving God's forgiveness.

### 17. Why do we need to tell the priest how long it has been since our last confession?

Typically, right after the penitent enters the confessional or reconciliation room, he or she is greeted by the priest with the words: "May the Lord be in your heart and on your lips so that you may worthily confess your sins, in the name of the Father, and of the Son, and of the Holy Spirit. Amen." At that point, the penitent begins, "Bless me, Father, for I have sinned. It has been [x weeks/months/years] since my last confession."

This information helps the confessor better understand how God's grace has been working in the penitent's spiritual life. It enables him to consider the following questions: Does the penitent need to confess more often? Is this confession part of a pattern of frequent confession and a sincere effort to amend one's moral and spiritual life? If the person has been away from the sacrament for many years, does he or she need encouragement to return to confession, as needed, sooner rather than later? If the person had just gone to confession a day or so earlier, does he or she have difficulty avoiding certain serious sins? These considerations form a context within which the priest can better understand the sins which are about to be confessed and advise the penitent more precisely.

18. **Does the penitent need to provide any other information to the priest before confessing his or her sins?**

A penitent does well to give the priest a general description of his or her state of life, i.e., whether the person is single, married, a religious sister or brother, or a priest. This information can help the priest better understand the context of the sins to be confessed and to guide the penitent in correcting wrong behavior. For example, in the case of sexual sins, the nature of the problem and the possible antidotes will vary for priests and religious, married, or single persons. This is true of many other types of sin, too. Advice from the priest and the assigned penance should be appropriate to the penitent's state of life.

**19. How does a person actually go about the confession of sins during the sacrament? How specific must one be in confessing his or her sins?**

Following a thorough examination of conscience, a person must confess each mortal sin that he or she can remember. Specify the type of each sin and, if possible, the definite number of times it was committed. In addition, any venial sins should also be confessed.

One should remember that the circumstances surrounding a particular sin bear a lot of weight in establishing its seriousness. For example, stealing to provide medicine for a dying child is far less egregious than simply stealing money for one's own use. Such circumstances should be mentioned to the priest so that he can offer the proper counsel and prescribe the appropriate penance.

**20. What is an "examination of conscience"?**

In the words of the *Catechism,* "Conscience is a judgment of reason by which the human person recognizes the moral quality of a concrete act" (CCC 1796). An examination of conscience is an honest personal assessment of one's sins of commission and omission, that is, the immoral acts that a person has committed or the moral duties that he or she has failed to fulfill. We are asked to make an examination of conscience before we go to confession (see CCC 1454). A suggested guideline for an examination of conscience can be found on page 90.

**21. Is there an "official" examination of conscience I should use?**

No. Rather, there are various ways to make a good examination of conscience, one which aids a person to reflect thoroughly and honestly on his or her actions, thoughts, or omissions before God. A good examination of conscience can be based on Sacred Scripture, beginning with the Ten Commandments (Ex 20:2-17; Dt 5:6-21) and the Beatitudes (Mt 5:3-11). In addition, there is great benefit in reflecting on other texts of Scripture, such as the Sermon on the Mount (Mt 5-7) or one of the moral exhortations from St. Paul's letters (e.g., Rom 12-15; Gal 4:12-6:10). Also, there are several excellent books to help examine one's conscience using a series of questions, including *How to Make a Good Confession* by John A. Kane (Sophia Institute Press, 2001).

Well-written examinations of conscience help remind us not only of the particular sins we may have committed, but also about other aspects of our lives and attitudes that we may not be immediately aware of, things which need to be addressed if we are to grow in holiness.

**22.  Is it necessary to confess every serious sin we have committed since our last confession, including the number of times each was done?**

Yes. A penitent must confess every mortal sin he remembers committing since his last confession, even if these sins are "most secret and have been committed against the last two precepts of the Decalogue [which forbid coveting the wife or goods of one's neighbor]" (CCC 1456). Why is this necessary? Because, unless a person enumerates his or her serious sins, the priest cannot use the authority given by Christ to forgive or to retain these sins. While it is spiritually fruitful to confess venial sins as well, it is not absolutely required to confess them individually, since venial sins do not exclude one from God's grace. Venial sins can be remitted in other ways, such as attendance at Mass and practicing works of charity, prayer, and penance (see CCC 1458).

**23.  What if one forgets to confess a particular sin?**

If a person truly forgets to confess a sin, it is considered forgiven. However, if it is subsequently remembered and is a mortal sin, the penitent must confess it the next time he or she goes to the sacrament of reconciliation.

**24.  What happens if you intentionally omit a particular sin in making a confession?**

Intentionally omitting a mortal sin is itself a serious sin, resulting in another mortal sin on one's conscience.

Someone who intentionally tries to hide an offence in confession is not pardoned. As the *Catechism*, quoting from the Council of Trent, notes, "When Christ's faithful strive to confess all the sins that they can remember, they undoubtedly place all of them before the divine mercy for pardon. But those who fail to do so and knowingly withhold some, place nothing before the divine goodness for remission through the mediation of the priest, 'for if the sick person is too ashamed to show his wound to the doctor, the medicine cannot heal what it does not know'" (CCC 1456).

In such a case, a person must repeat the confession, confessing the sin of purposely omitting confession of a serious sin and also the particular sin that was previously omitted.

### 25. Why do we need contrition in order to be forgiven?

As the *Catechism* states, "Among the penitent's acts contrition occupies the first place. Contrition is 'sorrow of the soul and detestation for the sin committed, together with the resolution not to sin again'" (CCC 1451). Sin is setting one's own will in opposition to God's will, and true repentance is a prerequisite for healing the sin-sick soul and being reconciled with God and His Church. As it says in one of the penitential psalms, "A broken and contrite heart, O God, you will not despise" (Ps 51:17). Contrition implies a turning away from sin and the resolution to begin a new life, along with a confidence in God's mercy and the desire to do what is necessary to receive the sacrament or reconciliation properly.

**26.  What is the difference between perfect and imperfect contrition?**

Perfect contrition is rooted in a love of God above all things. This kind of contrition is so powerful that it "reconciles man to God before this sacrament is actually received," though this reconciliation must include the desire for the sacrament of reconciliation (see CCC 1452).

Imperfect contrition (also known as *attrition*) is rooted in an appreciation of the ugliness of sin and in the fear of punishment, both in this life and eternally in hell. It is not as powerful spiritually as contrition that is motivated solely by love of God. Nonetheless, attrition "renounces the desire to sin and hopes for pardon." It is "a gift of God ... an impulse of the Holy Spirit" which prepares the penitent's soul for God's justice, without yet being the indwelling of God which moves a person to true love of God. Imperfect contrition requires the penitent to receive the sacrament of reconciliation in order to be justified before God, yet it disposes the person to receive God's sanctifying grace in this sacrament. Though imperfect, attrition is nonetheless an actual grace from God which can begin more profound activity in the human spirit (CCC 1453).

## 27. What is an "act of contrition" and why do we need to make one before we receive absolution from our sins?

An "act of contrition" is a prayer in which the penitent expresses his sorrow for past sins and declares his love for God and his intention not to sin again. This prayer is spoken aloud by the penitent following the confession of sins and prior to the priest's proclamation of absolution. The Church allows penitents to express their contrition in a variety of prayers. Some acts of contrition are simple, such as: "Lord Jesus, have mercy on me, a sinner." The traditional form expresses both perfect and imperfect contrition:

> O my God, I am heartily sorry for having offended You, and I detest all my sins because of Your just punishments, but most of all because they offend You, who are all good and deserving of all my love. I firmly resolve, with the help of Your grace, to sin no more and to avoid the near occasions of sin. Amen.

This prayer expresses sorrow and a total rejection of sin because of the fear of the just punishment that sin deserves (imperfect contrition). However, it goes further by recalling that God is all good, an even greater motive for sorrow because the penitent's sins have offended the divine majesty. Finally, the penitent makes a resolution not only to avoid sin but also those near occasions of sin that can lead to temptations. Keeping this resolution is possible not through one's own efforts alone, but only with the help of God's grace. A Scriptural model for an act of contrition is Psalm 51, which may also be read or meditated on for deeper understanding of contrition.

## 28. Why does the priest give us a penance to do?

The Church instructs priests to impose a penance as a form of satisfaction for the sins confessed. Sin has two consequences: the punishment which is due because of justice, and the stain of the sin which remains on the sinner's soul. Christ's death brings the forgiveness of sin and satisfies for the eternal punishment that is due for mortal sins. However, the stain of a person's sins may still remain, affecting the sinner and his relationship with God and others. Performing a penance can help cleanse the stain of sin and heal its effects. Some penances act as antidotes to the particular sin, e.g., a verbally-aggressive person may do acts of kindness for anyone he has hurt.

The penitent is not limited to the "canonical" penance imposed by the priest. For example, a priest may impose a penance of saying a rosary, but the penitent could add one or two more rosaries as an additional self-imposed penance. This does not mean that the canonical penance was insufficient, but rather that the person senses a need for the cleansing effects of good actions, such as prayer or acts of charity and kindness to others.

## 29. Isn't performing a penance like trying to earn our way to heaven?

The Catholic Church firmly teaches that human beings cannot "earn their way to heaven." Salvation is the free gift of God's grace, made possible by the passion, death, and resurrection of His Son, Jesus Christ (see CCC 161-162). The performance of a penance after confession is concerned with an issue traditionally identified as "satisfaction" for sin. Satisfaction refers to the payment of a debt. When applied to human sin, only Jesus, the God-Man, can pay the full debt of human sin, because He is both human and divine. Sharing our human nature, He can take upon Himself the debt of human sin. As God, He can make up for the full force of sin, which offends the infinite and all-good God. Since an offense acquires its seriousness according to the status of the person offended, human sins against God bear an infinite weight. Therefore, only an infinite person—that is, God—can take on the full burden of paying for such an offense. Human beings are by nature incapable of paying the infinite debt of sin which is incurred by offending the infinite God.

In fact, the acts of penance performed by a repentant sinner are efficacious solely due to of the merits of Christ's passion and death (see CCC 1460). Since a Christian is joined to Christ in baptism and becomes a member of His mystical body, the Church (see 1 Cor 12), he or she can share in His merits through union with Him. Our actions have no saving merit apart from Christ.

**30. If the effectiveness of penance comes from union with Jesus Christ and His merits, then why bother to perform any type of satisfaction?**

One way the penitent finds help is by investing himself in the process of making satisfaction for sin.

While Christ's merits are the truly effective elements in satisfaction for sin, the sinner receives deeper healing of the effects of sin by taking a personal share in making satisfaction in union with Christ. Some disobedient children may try to get away with simply saying, "I'm sorry," without understanding the consequences of their actions. They need to experience their parents' punishment and discipline to learn otherwise. In a similar way, repentant sinners need to learn the seriousness of their deeds by doing a penance—a punishment—imposed by the priest.

**31. What if you forget to do the penance that the confessor assigns?**

Forgetting to perform the assigned penance is not a sin, nor is it a sin to go to communion after inadvertently omitting the penance. It would only be sinful to refuse to perform the imposed penance consciously and willfully. Forgetfulness is simply one of the weaknesses of our fallen human nature. If you later remember the penance, you should do it immediately so as to begin forming a good habit.

**32. What if you forget what the priest gave you as a penance?**

Due to strong emotions that may be experienced during confession or simply a moment of distraction, you may not remember the particular penance imposed by the priest. While it not strictly required, you may return to the confessional to ask the priest the penance he gave. If this is not possible (for instance, if there is a line of people waiting for confession), try to remember the penance the best you can. Also, if you find yourself forgetting the penance on several occasions, it is a good idea to repeat it back to the priest before leaving the confessional or reconciliation room.

### 33. How does a priest know that a particular penance is sufficient to atone for a person's sins?

Remember that the atonement for sins has been won by the passion, death, and resurrection of Jesus (see CCC 614). The penance done by a repentant sinner has merit insofar as it unites him more closely with the sufferings of the Redeemer and makes him more Christ-like (see CCC 618, 1459-1460).

The priest is required to impose a penance based on three virtues: justice, prudence, and piety. Regarding justice, the priest needs to impose a penance which fits the seriousness of the sin committed. The penance for committing murder obviously should be more severe than that for speaking uncharitably about another. Justice also requires that the penitent be capable of performing the penance. For example, a priest cannot expect an illiterate person to read a passage from the Bible as a penance.

Prudence in imposing penances recognizes that a certain prayer or penitential act will truly help the person improve his or her moral and spiritual life. For instance, imposing an act of generosity on a husband who has argued with his wife will help heal the relationship.

Piety comes into play when a penance directs the penitent to a greater love of God, especially through prayer and reading Sacred Scripture.

The penitent can be confident that the canonical penance imposed by the priest is satisfactory based on the authority given him by Christ's Church. Persons who want to do additional penance may do so, but they should consult with a spiritual director or confessor, lest they be misled by an ill-advised spiritual enthusiasm. Such a misdirected enthusiasm can originate from a lack of confidence in Christ's mercy and His infinite satisfaction for sin, leading persons to fall into the heresy that they need to redeem themselves (i.e., Pelagianism).

## 34. How often should a Catholic go to confession?

According to the *Code of Canon Law*, Catholics, after having reached the age of reason (i.e., about age seven), are bound to confess serious sins at least once a year (see CCC 1457). Traditionally, this is done during the Lenten or Easter seasons. Similarly, Catholics are required to receive holy communion at least once a year, during the same liturgical season. This is traditionally called the "Easter Duty."

However, the Church recommends more frequent use of the sacrament of reconciliation, even if only for the forgiveness of venial sins. Automobile engines run smoother if they have regular tune-ups by a mechanic, and teeth stay healthier if they are cleaned regularly by a dentist. So, too, the spiritual life of the soul benefits from frequent confession. While the Church makes no specific requirement as to frequency, monthly or even weekly confession is recommended, especially if a person is struggling with a sinful habit. The grace of this sacrament is a powerful aid to overcoming temptation and helps heal the effects of each fall into sin.

**35. Can a particular celebration of the sacrament of reconciliation be invalid?**

Yes. If a person confesses a sin without being truly sorry for the sin committed, without a firm resolution not to sin again or without intending to perform the penance, the sacramental absolution is invalid. Furthermore, if a penitent has stolen property and refuses to make restitution for the theft, he or she cannot validly be absolved from this sin.

For the sacrament to be valid, the priest must be validly ordained and must also have *faculties* to hear confessions (that is, a delegated authority granted by the local bishop or religious superior). However, if the penitent is in danger of death, any priest—even a priest who has formally left the active priesthood or who does not possess Church-approved faculties—can validly grant absolution, provided that the penitent is truly sorry for his or her sins (see CIC, canon 976).

**36. Why is it that only a priest can grant us absolution from our sins?**

As noted previously, only a validly-ordained priest who has faculties granted by the local ordinary (the bishop or major religious superior) can hear confessions (except in the case of immediate danger of death).

Why is this, though? The *Catechism* explains it very eloquently: "Since Christ entrusted to his apostles the ministry of reconciliation, bishops who are their successors, and priests, the bishops' collaborators, continue to exercise this ministry" (CCC 1461).

The qualified and approved priest may be compared to an ambassador who has the authority to conduct a king's business in his absence. The ambassador is not the king, but he effectively takes the king's place in a foreign land, unless the king personally appears. The priest has "ambassadorial" authority to hear confessions and absolve sins for Jesus Christ, the King. This very image is used in 2 Corinthians 5:18-20:

> All this is from God, who through Christ reconciled us to himself and gave us the ministry of reconciliation; that is, in Christ God was reconciling the world to himself, not counting their trespasses against them, and entrusting to us the message of reconciliation. So we are ambassadors for Christ, God making his appeal through us. We beseech you on behalf of Christ, be reconciled to God.

### 37.  What is the "seal of confession" I've heard about?

The *seal of confession* refers to the absolute requirement that a priest never reveal anything he hears during a person's confession. This refers to the sins confessed and any other matters discussed during the confession. Outside the confessional, a priest may not even speak to a penitent about confessed sins (unless the penitent brings them up of his own volition) or even indicate that he has heard a particular person's confession. As the *Catechism* notes, the sacramental seal "admits of no exceptions" (see CCC 1467)—even if what has been confessed concerns a criminal act (or the intention to commit a criminal act). The *Code of Canon Law* (canon 983) states that the sacramental seal is inviolable, whether the person has been absolved of the sin or not. If the priest "breaks the seal" by disclosing a person's sin in any way, whether through words or other means, canon 983 calls this *nefas*, the Latin word for "criminal."

### 38. What happens if a priest "breaks the seal" and discloses what has been said in confession?

A priest who violates the seal of confession is subject to very severe ecclesiastical penalties. According to the *Code of Canon Law*, a priest who deliberately reveals a penitent's sins and identity is subject to an automatic (*latae sententiae*) excommunication, which can be lifted only by the Apostolic See, i.e., the Pope (see canon 1388).

### 39. Can a priest really be excommunicated for disclosing *anything* he hears in confession?

Not exactly. As previously noted, if the priest deliberately reveals a penitent's sins and identity, then he is automatically excommunicated according to canon 1388. If a priest's simple carelessness causes a penitent's sins or identity to become known, then the penalty he suffers can be adjusted to the seriousness of his deed. The punishment can be excommunication or a lesser penalty, such as losing his faculties to hear confessions or publicly celebrate the other sacraments.

## 40. What if a person tells a priest in confession that he plans on hurting—or even murdering—someone?

The sacramental seal is absolute. This means that *nothing* the priest hears from a penitent during a sacramental confession may be revealed—not even a penitent's plan to commit a crime such as murder. While this may sound extreme, even harmful to society, the absolute secrecy of the sacrament must be maintained. In such a case, the priest must refuse to give absolution since the person obviously does not repent of the sin that he or she is about to commit. However, even when the priest withholds absolution, the seal remains intact for anything revealed during a sacramental confession.

## 41. So a priest cannot tell the police about a planned crime which is revealed to him in confession?

No. Since the seal of confession permits no exceptions, a priest cannot disclose any information revealed during a confession to anyone—not even to the police, if it involves a criminal matter. The police need to do their own job of investigating crimes, without help from priests in the confessional.

Canon 984 mentions a similar but more common situation in the Church: a master of novices or a rector of a seminary or school who hears the confession of one of his students may not use that information obtained in confession in any way for the external governance of that person. The secrecy of the confessional is sacrosanct.

## 42. Are there any known cases in which a priest has revealed the contents of a confession?

Though such cases may have occurred over the two millennia of the Church's history, we have not been able to find any modern documented cases of a priest willfully breaking the seal of confession.

## 43. Have priests ever gotten into legal trouble due to their refusal to reveal a penitent's sins?

Yes. St. John Nepomucene (1340–1393) was tortured and then drowned by King Wenceslaus IV of Bohemia because he would not reveal the sins confessed by the queen. In 1813, a Jesuit priest from New York, Father Anthony Kohlman, S.J., was called into court to testify concerning matters he had learned about during a confession. When he refused to testify, Father Kohlman was tried for contempt of court. The issue was finally settled when the State of New York passed a law exempting priests from revealing any information obtained in confession.

In another episode, a simple French priest, Abbé Dumoulin, gave a large sum of money to a woman who was later found murdered at a nearby monastery. A knife dripping with her blood was found in the rectory kitchen. Abbé Dumoulin was arrested, convicted, and sent to prison in New Caledonia. However, after three years, the church sexton admitted that he had killed the woman for her money and confessed the crime to Abbé Dumoulin. Keeping the seal inviolable, this holy priest remained silent as a lamb led to slaughter until the sexton confessed his crime to the police. The French Supreme Court acquitted the priest and he returned to his overjoyed parish.

## 44. Does the seal of confession apply to anyone besides the priest?

Yes, it does. A penitent who does not speak the same language as the priest confessor may bring a translator into the confessional. In such a case, however, the translator is also bound by the seal of confession (see CIC, canon 983.2). The same canon says that anyone who accidentally or purposely overhears another person's confession is bound by the seal to keep it a secret, even from the penitent. Anyone who overhears another person's confession must keep this a secret under the seal of confession, under pain of serious sin. The penalties for revealing another person's confessional material must be just, according to the seriousness of the offense. The penalties may include excommunication, though this is not automatic as in the case of a priest who breaks the seal.

**45. Can I confess my sins over the phone if it is not convenient for me to get to the church when confessions are being heard?**

No, the sacrament of penance cannot be celebrated over the phone. Why? Simply because the telephone is not a secure medium; others may be able to tap into a phone call, whether on purpose or by accident, thus jeopardizing the seal of confession.

In 1996, there was a case in an Oregon prison, in which a priest heard a prisoner's confession over the visiting room phone because it was impossible to hear the prisoner's confession through the glass wall separating them. However, unbeknownst to the priest or the penitent, prison guards taped the confession. When prosecutors planned to use this recording during the man's trial, Church officials went to court to prevent this egregious violation of the seal of confession, ultimately winning their case against the state and preventing the taped confession from being used.

**46. Would it be possible to confess one's sins over the Internet and receive absolution?**

No. Confession over the Internet, whether by email or instant messaging, is not permitted for the same reason that phone confessions are not permitted. Email and instant messaging are not secure means of communication; there is always the possibility that the seal of confession could be violated by hackers. In addition, neither the priest nor the penitent could be certain that the other person is who he claims to be. So we should not expect the Church to set up an "Iconfess.com" website anytime soon.

### 47.  Is it possible to confess in advance a sin one plans to commit at a later date?

While one can certainly confess one's malicious intention to commit a sin, the actual sin cannot be forgiven before it has been committed. A person who states an intention to sin obviously does not have a firm resolution to avoid sin, which is one of the requirements for absolution. Such a person does not have a clear understanding of confession. For this reason the priest needs to warn such a person of the seriously bad moral state of his or her soul and try to discourage the sin and encourage virtue.

### 48.  Does the priest need to know a penitent's identity in order to able to administer the sacrament of reconciliation?

Not at all. Every penitent has the right to anonymity in confession (see CIC, canon 964.2). While reconciliation rooms have become common since the revision of the rite following the Second Vatican Council, such rooms must provide a screen through which a penitent can confess anonymously. As a further safeguard, every Catholic has the right to choose his or her confessor. According to canon 991, the penitent may even choose a priest who belongs to a different rite. (The term *rite* here refers to the different ecclesial communities within the Catholic Church, all of which are under the authority of the pope. The Roman Rite is the largest and the majority of the other rites have their origin in the Middle East or Eastern Europe, e.g., Melkite, Maronite, etc.).

## 49. Were the penances in the early Church harsher than those given today?

In order to understand the severity of the penances given in the early Church, one needs to know that sacramental confession was particularly reserved for a number of very serious sins: murder, adultery, fornication, apostasy (i.e., denying the faith), heresy, and betraying the sacred books or vessels (an important issue during the great persecutions). For such sins the penances were serious and very often publicly performed. Furthermore, the early Church had a different understanding of the connection between doing penance and receiving pardon. The Church would grant absolution after the confession of sin and the performance of the penance, since pardon was considered the fruit of doing penance.

Public penances for sin might include requiring the penitent to stand in front of the church from Ash Wednesday until Holy Thursday, wearing goat haircloth (a symbol of being counted with the goats rather than the sheep; see Mt 25:33) and covered with ashes. Only after the person performed a lengthy penance (sometimes lasting years) would he or she receive absolution. During the time of penance the person would not be permitted to receive holy communion.

## 50. Are there any sins which cannot be forgiven in confession? What about the "unforgivable sin" that Jesus speaks about?

First, let's clarify what exactly Jesus means by the unforgivable sin against the Holy Spirit, mentioned in Mark 3:28-29: "Truly, I say to you, all sins will be forgiven the sons of men, and whatever blasphemies they utter; but whoever blasphemes against the Holy Spirit never has forgiveness, but is guilty of an eternal sin."

Pope John Paul, in his 1986 encyclical on the Holy Spirit, *Dominum et Vivificantem*, writes that this sin does not merely consist of speaking blasphemous words against the Holy Spirit; rather, it is "the refusal to accept the salvation which God offers to man through the Holy Spirit, working through the power of the Cross." Human will is free to reject and stubbornly oppose God's mercy. As Saint Thomas Aquinas taught, it is a sin that is "unforgivable by its very nature" because it excludes the essential elements through which the forgiveness of sin takes place. For example, a person who despairs of forgiveness sins against the Holy Spirit because he is convinced that, "My sin is so bad, God could never forgive me." The essence of such a sin is an overweening pride that claims to have the power to commit a sin so great that even God could not forgive it; it is a disbelief in the mercy of God.

**51. If such a person repents of such a sin and then sincerely seeks forgiveness, is it too late for him to be forgiven?**

No, not at all. Only if such a person persists in this sin until death (i.e., final impenitence) would it be truly unforgivable. Until that moment, God is constantly sending the person actual grace to repent. If such a person repents, it is because the Holy Spirit has broken through the defenses of pride and has been able to convince him or her of the seriousness of the sin and the possibility of Christ's forgiveness.

**52. What if a person repeatedly confesses a serious sin committed once in the past and feels no peace no matter how many times he or she confesses it? Does this indicate the person has committed the unforgivable sin?**

While it certainly is a spiritual problem that the person does not experience any peace after repeatedly confessing the same sin, such a reaction does not indicate the presence of the "unforgivable sin" against the Holy Spirit. Rather, the person's conscience is troubled by something else. For instance, a person may not feel capable of making sufficient restitution for the sin, or, if true restitution is not possible, they yearn for a way to make reparation. Rather than repeatedly confessing the sin which had been already confessed in previous sacramental confessions, the person should look for a more positive method of making an act of reparation. For instance, a thief may do extra penance by giving a portion of his income to charity or perform acts of caring for the weak and needy. This does not mean that the canonical penance imposed by the priest in the original confession was insufficient to reconcile the person with God and the Church. However, a continuing lack of peace indicates a deeper need for reconciliation and healing of the pain caused by their sin. This applies to the pain caused in others as well as within their own souls.

### 53. If a person intentionally does not confess a particular sin, is that sin also an "unforgivable sin"?

No, it is not *unforgivable*, but it may remain *unforgiven*. God does not reconcile a sinner who intentionally omits a particular sin in making his confession. If the unconfessed sin is mortal in nature, then it remains unforgiven until the penitent confesses it, along with the additional sin of purposefully concealing a mortal sin. If the penitent simply forgets to confess it, the sin is actually forgiven during confession, but the person needs to mention it the next time they celebrate the sacrament of reconciliation. Thus, a sin that is purposely concealed or accidentally forgotten is definitely a forgivable sin. An unforgivable sin is one which by its very nature is not capable of being forgiven; this does not apply to sins which have not yet been forgiven.

### 54. Are there any situations in which a priest might refuse to absolve someone?

Jesus Christ gave the apostles the power to "bind and loose," to forgive sins or retain them (see Jn 20:23). This authority was passed on to their successors, the bishops, and to priests. So priests have the ability to withhold absolution from a sinner for a just cause, though the situations in which they would do so are rare.

In question 48 we discussed the case of a person declaring in confession that he or she intends to commit a sin in the future. Furthermore, an unmarried man who confesses the sin of fornication but refuses to give up cohabitating with his girlfriend would be denied absolution, simply because he has not demonstrated a firm purpose of amendment. Any situation where a person refuses to make a firm resolve to repent of sin and avoid doing it again is one in which a priest can and should refuse absolution.

## 55. Can a priest refuse to hear a person's confession?

Only for a serious reason, but this would be unusual. For instance, if a priest has a pressing ministerial obligation, such as celebrating Mass, he may delay hearing a person's confession until after Mass. Though some penitents may have a legitimate urgency which could cause a priest to change his schedule, normally one should respect a priest's plans and work out some reasonable accommodation.

Another situation would be that of a priest who knows that a penitent is ineligible to receive the sacraments, including confession. This would be the case when someone is penalized with *interdict*, a public declaration which excludes a person from receiving the sacraments as a penalty for some very grievous sin. Such a situation, however, is extremely rare.

## 56. Does a priest remember the sins that a particular person confesses?

Nearly every priest will tell you that he rarely remembers the sins confessed by a particular person. There are several reasons for this: 1) the sheer number of confessions he hears in a given week or month; 2) the fact that nearly everyone confesses a variation of the same sins, making it difficult to connect a particular sin with a specific person; and 3) the grace of holy orders in ministering this sacrament. In addition, the burden of forgiving sin depends on the sacrificial death of Christ on the cross, not on a priest's memory. Furthermore, since a priest cannot speak to anyone about the sins he hears in confession, he has no reason to remember them.

Of course, when a penitent regularly confesses face-to-face to his or her spiritual director, a priest in that situation may indeed remember the particular sins and issues the person is dealing with. This is actually helpful in providing more fruitful counsel and direction. If the penitent brings up previously confessed matters, the priest is free to speak about them to the penitent during confession in order to help the person make moral progress and grow stronger in the Christian life.

**57.  I prefer to go to confession anonymously, but I'm afraid that my pastor will recognize my voice and I'll be embarrassed when I see him.**

Such a fear is unfounded. Even if your pastor recognizes your voice, there is no reason to be embarrassed when you next see him—for the simple reason that, as we discussed in the previous answer, he almost certainly does not remember the sins you confessed. Also, priests will tell you that one of the joys of hearing confession is granting absolution. Reconciling someone to God in the sacrament of reconciliation gives great peace and joy to a priest, who is always concerned for a penitent's spiritual welfare. The last thing he intends is to cause a penitent any embarrassment.

**58.  If the priest does not remember my sins, does God remember them?**

God, being omniscient, has a perfect knowledge of reality. In addition, He is eternal, existing outside of space and time. Everything to Him is "eternally present." So, strictly speaking, it is impossible for Him to "forget" anything. Every sin and virtuous deed remains present to Him for all eternity. Thus, the important thing is not whether God "remembers" our sin; rather, it is to turn away from sin and seek reconciliation with Him, to live a life of grace and virtue.

**59.** **What about a person who is stuck in a habit of sin and knows that he will not be able to change his life immediately. Could a priest refuse him absolution?**

By their very nature, habitual sins are difficult to overcome. When a person has developed a habit of sin and does his best to reform, but is still unable to avoid a certain sin, a priest may certainly grant absolution, provided that the person makes a firm resolution to amend his life and takes the best steps he can to correct his behavior and avoid temptation.

Many people struggle with habitual sins, the most common being in the areas of sexuality, eating, gambling, compulsive shopping, and gossip, among others. While they may strive with all their might to overcome a particular habit, they may still fail on occasion. Every time they fail, such people should seek reconciliation by going to confession. They should not become discouraged (as discouragement is always from the devil) but should have faith that Christ's grace in the sacrament will, in time, help them change bad habits into good ones.

Some people struggle with addictions to drugs or alcohol. A true addiction, of course, limits a person's ability to make a free choice and, thus, mitigates their responsibility for each time they become intoxicated. Since such dependency has physical, psychological, emotional, and spiritual components, the grace of the sacrament of reconciliation (along with psychological counseling and treatment) will be very helpful in their efforts to be freed from their addiction.

## 60. If God only forgives us if we are truly sorry for our sins, then why should I forgive someone who has offended me and yet is not sorry?

While it is true that we need to be truly sorry for our sins in order to have them forgiven, we need to remember that God has reconciled all of us to Himself through the death and resurrection of His Son, Jesus. We simply need to accept this reconciliation and let His grace work in our lives. The very fact that we are in a position to receive God's forgiveness in the first place is a monumental reality. In Luke 23:34, Jesus said, "Father, forgive them; for they know not what they do." Jesus not only asked the Father to forgive His torturers and executioners while they were taunting him, He even offered an excuse for their wicked behavior: "they know not what they do."

The reason why we have to be sorry for our sins and seek God's forgiveness is because these are the steps necessary for us to receive and accept the reconciliation that God has already accomplished by Christ's death on the cross.

In asking us to forgive people who have offended us, even before they are sorry for their misdeeds, God is asking us to do what He has already done. In this way, we share in the mystery of reconciliation, sometimes by sharing in the pain and sadness of forgiving people who do not want to be forgiven, who may not believe they are responsible for anything bad or who simply refuse to love us. At this point, we imitate God, whose mercy exceeds mere fairness or strict justice. Yet we do so following the beatitude, "Blessed are the merciful, for they shall obtain mercy" (Mt 5:7).

**61. I know Catholics who continue to commit public sins, go to confession, and receive holy communion on Sunday as if they were good people. This seems hypocritical to me.**

We need to be very careful when judging another person from appearances. As Jesus warns us, "Judge not, that you may not be judged. For with the judgment you pronounce will you be judged, and the measure you give will be the measure you get" (Mt 7:1-2). We do not know what is in another person's heart, nor do we know the state of someone else's soul before God. All we can do is observe their external behavior or listen to what they reveal to us. So we really cannot accuse someone of being a hypocrite unless they publicly condemn others for committing the same sins.

**62. Why do fewer Catholics go to confession today than a generation ago?**

Since there are no Nielsen ratings for confession, we cannot say how many penitents confessed recently. It is true, however, that the number of people in confession lines has declined over the past forty years in nearly every parish church in the United States.

There are a number of reasons for this decline. One is that the number of sermons on sin, purgatory, hell, and the need to be well-prepared to face the judgment of God have become less common in our modern age than they were a generation or two ago. As a result, Catholics do not think as often about these issues and the need to go to confession regularly.

In addition, some penitents have reported being put off by the actions or demeanor of certain priests. One priest expressed indignation upon learning that a penitent had come to confession more than once in a month. In some places, the local parish does not regularly schedule time for confessions, requiring all penitents to make personal appointments with one of the priests to receive the sacrament. While experiences such as these understandably explain why some have been "turned off" from confession, we need to remember that the important thing is being reconciled with God and the Church; we should not let the bad example of a few priests get in the way of our spiritual good.

Our secular culture influences many people by claiming that certain actions—particularly in the sexual realm—are not sinful. Others say that since everyone is committing these sins, God could not send everyone to hell, so do not break ranks and start confessing. This is a group insurance plan without any capital to back up its claims. Similarly, some people say, "I'm not a bad person; I haven't killed anyone." To which one of the authors (Fr. Pacwa) generally replies, "You seem to be a good person, so long as you are comparing yourself to Al Capone. Once the norm for behavior is Jesus Christ, the evaluation may change."

## 63. Isn't confession just a crutch for the weak-minded and superstitious?

No. Confession is not some Jedi mind trick or an opiate for the weak-minded. First, an examination of conscience, a necessary preparation for confession, requires clear thinking, true self-knowledge, humility, and the courage to admit one's responsibility for personal sin. Weak-minded individuals do not normally think through moral issues or display the virtue of courage very often.

Superstitious people believe that an amulet or magic formula can be used to conform reality to their own desires. In confession, penitents realize their failures in conforming to God's moral and spiritual expectations, take responsibility for these failures, and ask God to forgive them as a free gift, not in response to a command from a human mind.

If anything, confession is an antidote to weak-mindedness, precisely because it directly confronts weakness of the will. It is an antidote to superstition because it acknowledges the power of God to reconcile us with Him through the free gift of Christ's saving death on the cross. The result is that confession elevates sinners to a higher plane of mature relationship with God.

## 64. Why are some people afraid of going to confession?

Some people fear the embarrassment associated with putting one's sins into words and telling another person (a priest) their most personal and secret actions. They may have difficulty making themselves vulnerable to a priest by verbally expressing their sins, fearing that the priest will yell at them or feel revulsion towards them as a result of the sins they have confessed. Some may even fear that the priest will refuse to absolve them of their sins.

Over the years, some movies—for comedic effect—have portrayed priests becoming enraged at penitents and lashing out at them verbally or even physically. Such films, though fictional exaggerations, play upon the fears and insecurities some Catholics have about going to confession.

Still others may fear that another person may overhear their confession, or, as also appears in some movies, they may mistakenly confess to someone who is not a priest.

Those who wrestle with such unfounded fears should pray to God for the grace to overcome them. The powerful spiritual effect of reconciliation is so necessary and positive a good that no fears should be allowed to prevent anyone from experiencing it.

## 65. Are there any other spiritual benefits from confession besides receiving the forgiveness of our sins?

First, one should not underestimate the many other benefits and graces that come from having one's sins forgiven and being in good standing with God. Second, since an examination of conscience is a prerequisite to making a good confession, confession helps us gain thorough knowledge of ourselves, especially of our moral weaknesses. This helps us to work on these weaknesses and repair our relationship with God and with others whom we have hurt and offended by our sins. Third, the profound spiritual and emotional peace one feels after receiving absolution is a tremendous benefit in a world that is frequently torn by turmoil and unrest. The noted psychiatrist Carl Jung claimed that fewer than five percent of his patients were practicing Catholics, and he speculated that this was due to the deep, therapeutic value of confession.

**66.   I feel great when I come out of confession. Is this feeling truly spiritual or is it merely psychological?**

To answer this question, it is necessary to distinguish the spiritual life from mere psychological states and emotions. Since the human spirit is that aspect of the person in which God communes at the deepest levels, emotions and feelings are not proper to the spirit. Emotions are those wonderful or frightening reactions which the body makes manifest in a variety of ways (e.g., laughter, tears, anxiety, etc.). These emotions, along with thoughts and acts of the will, are components of human psychology.

When a person experiences a true spiritual renewal—such as occurs in confession—this renewal is accompanied by a change in one's thoughts, will, and emotions. Spiritual renewal and conversion is more profound and long-lasting than merely psychological or emotional healing because it involves God's gracious mercy and forgiveness. However, such a conversion is often accompanied by a positive feelings (though not always and not necessarily to the same degree). One can enjoy the spiritual "peace that surpasses understanding" (Phil 4:7) because it goes beyond human thoughts and feelings. Nonetheless, feelings of peace and joy are quite common after confession. Even the priest often experiences feelings of joy at seeing penitents leave the confessional reconciled and strengthened in their walk with the Lord.

### 67. Do you think fewer Catholics would need psychological counseling if they went to confession more often?

Perhaps. Some psychological problems are related to a person's inability to deal with feelings of guilt and accept responsibility for his or her behavior. As we have previously noted, famous psychiatrist Carl Jung claimed that fewer than five percent of his patients were practicing Catholics, attributing such a small percentage to the therapeutic qualities of confession.

We must be careful, though, not to overstate confession's role as preventive medicine for psychological issues. Some psychological problems have their roots in physiological disorders and deficiencies (e.g., schizophrenia, bipolar disorder, etc.) and have no direct connection to moral weakness or sin. Such disorders are rightly treated by medication and psychiatric counseling. Others, who do not suffer from such psychiatric disorders, may simply need to discuss their fears, problems, and inner conflicts with a professional therapist. Such psychological counseling is not the material for confession because it often is unrelated to admission of guilt and the reception of reconciliation with God and others. It is more accurate to say that confession and counseling can be mutually complementary while remaining distinct from each other.

## 68. What is spiritual direction?

Spiritual direction is the opportunity for a Christian to meet privately with a *spiritual director* (usually a priest, deacon, or a religious brother or sister, but possibly even a lay person who is trained in pastoral counseling) to discuss one's prayer life, spiritual growth, and the discernment of God's will for one's life.

Spiritual direction differs from psychological counseling in several ways: First, spiritual direction seeks to help a person discern the direction God is leading him or her, whether it be to a particular vocation or to a specific direction in one's apostolic service. It helps a believer to answer the question, "How can I discover the vocation to which God is calling me, whether to marriage, the priesthood, or religious life?"

Second, spiritual direction addresses issues in a person's prayer life, focusing on such questions as: "How can I grow closer to God in prayer?", "Is there a particular method of prayer that would help me better than another?", and "How do periods of consolation or desolation affect my prayer life?"

Third, spiritual direction focuses on an individual's growth in the virtues. In this respect, one may ask, "How can I overcome a particular sin or bad habit?", "How do I advance in the theological virtues of faith, hope and charity?", "What should I do to aid my growth in the cardinal virtues of prudence, justice, fortitude, and temperance?"

Although psychological concerns may affect these three areas of the spiritual life, they are still quite distinct from it. Psychological counseling, in contrast to spiritual direction, seeks to address issues that are psychological or emotional in nature, e.g., overcoming a particular trauma, addiction, or disorder.

**69. How is confession different from spiritual direction?**

The primary concern of confession is one's admission of guilt, the determination to sin no more, the reception of absolution from the priest, and doing penance (i.e., making satisfaction) for one's sins, although one may occasionally receive some spiritual counsel from the priest during confession.

Whereas confession focuses on the remedial aspect of removing sin and restoring the life of grace in a soul, spiritual direction focuses on a person's positive growth in grace through prayer, the discernment of God's will in concrete circumstances, and progress in practicing the virtues. As such, confession and spiritual direction are distinct but complementary.

## 70. How should one go about choosing a spiritual director?

A number of factors should guide a person in choosing a suitable spiritual director. The first is interpersonal compatibility, which allows for comfort and ease in speaking about one's spiritual life, the most intimate aspect of human existence. It may help to have certain shared experiences, such as common interests and background, though this does not play as important a role as one might initially think.

A second issue is a spiritual director's theological training, since a sound understanding of the dynamics of the spiritual life is essential in guiding another person in his or her walk with God and growth in holiness.

A third issue is the quality of the potential director's experience. Is he or she personally familiar with the spiritual life? Does he or she have a sound prayer life? Has he or she had experience in giving direction to others? A key quality to watch for is the ability of the director to let God take the lead in one's spiritual life, with the director serving as a guide and staying out of God's way.

## 71. Should I use the same criteria for choosing a confessor?

If you mean a regular confessor, i.e., a priest with whom you celebrate the sacrament of reconciliation on a regular basis, then the criteria for choosing a good spiritual director can also apply. Knowledge of the spiritual life, intelligence, wisdom, and compatibility are good qualities to seek in a confessor. However, one's sins can certainly be forgiven by any priest, regardless of his personal abilities or virtues (or the lack thereof). We should always remember that it is Jesus Himself who acts through the priest in forgiving sins by the power of His death and resurrection. Furthermore, as the *Code of Canon Law* points out, every penitent has the right to choose any confessor he or she wants (see CIC, canon 991).

**72. If my spiritual director is also my confessor, can he bring up during spiritual direction sins that I previously confessed?**

A priest who is both confessor and spiritual director must take care to keep the two roles distinct. He cannot discuss the particular sins told to him during confession unless the directee brings them up. Therefore, a spiritual director should let his directee know at the outset of their relationship that discussion of confessional matter must be initiated by the directee. Thus, outside of confession, a spiritual director may not probe with such questions as: "How is the gossiping going?" or "Have you stopped having lustful thoughts?" Such an investigation could damage the trust that should exist in spiritual direction and would, strictly speaking, violate the seal of confession. This is why the *Code of Canon Law* prohibits directors of novices and rectors of seminaries from hearing the confessions of their novices or students unless the students themselves request it (see CIC, canon 985).

### 73. If a person commits a sin with a priest, can he or she confess that sin to the same priest?

If this sin involves a sexual matter, absolutely not. As the 1983 *Code of Canon Law* makes clear, it is forbidden to give absolution to an accomplice in a sin against the sixth commandment (see CIC, canon 977). The 1917 *Code*, though, applied this principle to any sin against any commandment committed by a priest with an accomplice, including stealing, bearing false witness, etc. Since the 1983 *Code* limits this principle to sexual sin, this must be understood as the current legal definition. A confession heard by an accomplice in sexual sin is invalid, except in the danger of death.

### 74. If two priests conspire to sin together, can they absolve each other?

No. Again, canon 977 would apply to each of the priests who acted as accomplices in committing a sin. Each would need to confess to a priest who was not at all involved in the offense.

### 75. At what age do Catholics begin going to confession?

The *Catechism* (CCC 1457) and the *Code of Canon Law* (CIC, canon 989) state the rule that a baptized Catholic should begin to receive the sacrament of reconciliation at the "age of discretion." This is also commonly referred to as the "age of reason," i.e., when a child becomes able to distinguish right from wrong. The child needs to have learned the Ten Commandments and the rudiments of other moral laws appropriate for his or her level of development, be able to remember past sins, understand that they are wrong because they offend God, and know that he or she can turn to Jesus for forgiveness. The age of discretion develops around age seven, but parents and teachers may discern a somewhat earlier or later development in certain children.

**76. Is it right to burden children with such negative ideas as sin and hell?**

As Jesus repeatedly makes clear in the Gospel, sin and hell are realities. So, of course, it is necessary to instruct children about them. Morbid, detailed descriptions of horrific punishments in hell are not appropriate, unless giving kids nightmares is one's cruel goal. However, parents and other responsible adults do right in warning younger children about the consequences of their misbehavior in the home. As they get older, it is their responsibility also to warn children about the consequences of breaking civil law, such as being sentenced by a juvenile court to prison or to do community service. It is just as important a responsibility to warn children about hell, which is the ultimate and most serious consequence of sin. Those who teach these truths must be prudent in making the connections between sin and punishment, as well as being moderate in their descriptions of hell.

## 77.  How often should children go to confession?

In the not-too-distant past, monthly confession was common in parochial schools. As the *Catechism* and the *Code of Canon Law* indicate, children must make their first confession before they make their first holy communion (see CIC, canon 914; CCC 1457). Then, as they begin to commit various sins, they would be well instructed to go to confession on a regular basis. This develops in them a good habit of examining their consciences, accepting responsibility for their misdeeds, and doing penance for their sins.

## 78.  Can children really commit serious sins that need to be confessed?

Yes, they can. Though some people may have an idealized view of children's innocence, as Christians we must always remember that every child bears the effects of original sin, i.e., that they are born into a fallen world. So children can—and do—commit serious sins. In recent decades, we have seen news reports of children in various countries committing horrific acts, such as murder. Though relatively rare, such crimes are occasionally committed by children, perhaps partly because they see them portrayed in the media or in their home environment.

In addition, some actions, when done by a child, are more serious in nature than if the same actions were done by an adult. Children might try an adult behavior (say, taking the car for a drive or playing with real guns), and this becomes a serious sin, not only because the parents forbid it, but also because such an act seriously endangers the child and others.

Finally, some deliberate acts of selfishness, lying, and disobedience can be serious sins which confession may help to remedy.

**79. When I was young, everyone went to confession behind a screen in a "confessional box." Now we can go face to face in a "reconciliation room." What was the reason for this change?**

Prior to the promulgation of the revised Rite of Penance in 1973, the custom and law of the Catholic Church was to celebrate confession in confessionals so that the priest would be publicly available while protecting the penitent's anonymity. In 1974, though, the National Conference of Catholic Bishops (now the USCCB), using the permission given them in the revised Roman Ritual, allowed priests to hear confessions in small chapels or reconciliation rooms. The purpose was to offer a more informal way of hearing confessions and an exchange of spiritual counsel (see Bishops' Committee on the Liturgy Newsletter, December 1974, p. 450). However, such reconciliation chapels were supposed to make both options available: face-to-face confession and the anonymity of a screen between the priest and the penitent. The penitent, not the priest, has the right to choose confessing face-to-face. According to the Pontifical Council for the Interpretation of Legislative Texts, however, a priest may choose to hear confessions only behind a screen:

If, according to Canon 964, paragraph 2, of the *Code of Canon Law*, the minister of the sacrament, for a just cause and excluding cases of necessity, can legitimately decide, even in the eventuality that the penitent ask for the contrary, that sacramental confession be received in a confessional with a fixed grille (July 24, 1998).

## 80. When can we go to confession? Are there special times?

It is customary for parishes to have regularly scheduled times for confession, traditionally on Saturday afternoons. Many parishes also have confession during the week, either before daily Masses or on a particular night, so that the sacrament is widely available. Of course, one can go to confession any time a priest is available. Common courtesy usually requires that one call the rectory and make an appointment, so that the priest's schedule and prior obligations might be respected. In an emergency or a true crisis of conscience, though, one may seek out a priest by simply knocking on the rectory door or stopping him after Mass.

Some shrines and monasteries have confession available on a daily basis for longer periods of time. Catholics are free to go to confession at any church, shrine, or monastery.

## 81. How often are Catholics required to go to confession?

The Church requires Catholics to go to confession at least once a year, if they are conscious of having committed a mortal sin (see CIC, canon 989). If a person has not committed any serious sins, then this obligation does not apply. Traditionally, this minimum of annual confession is done during the Lenten and Easter seasons so that he or she can celebrate the Paschal season, the high point of the Church's liturgical year, by receiving holy communion. Of course, anyone who is in the state of mortal sin may not receive holy communion until he or she repents of the sin and confesses it in the sacrament of reconciliation.

**82. Are non-Catholics allowed to go to confession in the Catholic Church?**

Ordinarily, non-Catholics are not permitted to receive any of the sacraments of the Church besides baptism (see CIC, canon 844, section 1). A member of an Eastern Orthodox Church (e.g., Greek Orthodox, Russian Orthodox, etc.), however, may receive the sacraments in a Catholic church if there is no Orthodox congregation nearby. The person must ask to receive the sacrament of his or her own accord and have proper dispositions of faith that Catholic sacraments are valid (see CIC, canon 844, section 3). A Protestant who is in danger of death, and who professes faith in the sacraments of the Church may go to confession and even receive holy communion and the anointing of the sick (see CIC, canon 844, section 4). Outside of these circumstances, non-Catholics would not be admitted to any sacrament, including confession. However, non-Catholics may certainly approach a priest for counsel, advice, and prayer. Many do so, in fact. This is always a ministry and service that any priest can do for any person.

It is appropriate to note here that a Catholic may receive the sacraments of penance, Eucharist, and anointing of the sick from non-Catholic ministers whose churches have valid sacraments, such as the Eastern Orthodox churches. The concern expressed in canon law is that the danger of error or indifferentism must be avoided and the need is real, such as when a person cannot go to a Catholic church (see CIC, canon 844, section 2). Keep in mind, many Eastern Orthodox priests may not accept the validity of Catholic sacraments, including baptism. While Catholics believe the Orthodox sacraments are valid, Orthodox priests may refuse the sacraments to a Catholic, so Catholics must respect their conscience on this point.

**83. If confession offers reconciliation with God, why does the Church teach that we may still need to suffer punishment for our confessed sins in purgatory?**

The Bible teaches that temporal punishment for sin may remain even after a person repents and is forgiven. For example, after their sin, Eve was punished with pain in childbirth and Adam with working by the sweat of his brow, and both would die, even after God showed them mercy (Gn 3:15-19). Three other episodes show that forgiven people still had to suffer temporal punishment while they lived on earth: Moses, who disobeyed God by tapping the rock instead of speaking to it to make water flow, was not allowed to enter the Promised Land (Nm 20:12), even though he was to be counted among the redeemed—as evidenced by His appearance with Christ at the Transfiguration (see Mt 17:3; Mk 9:4; Lk 9:30). A second episode occurs when the Israelites rebel and refuse to enter the Promised Land because they fear attacking the Canaanites. At Moses' pleading the Lord said, "I have pardoned, according to your word." However, God still punishes those He has pardoned by forbidding them "to see the land which I swore to give to their fathers" (Nm 14:13-23). A third episode occurs after Nathan announces pardon to David for his sins of adultery and murder, yet the punishment continues as David's son by Bathsheba dies a few days after birth and rebellion plagues David's family for years afterward (see 2 Sam 12).

Similarly, though the sacrament of reconciliation removes the eternal punishment due to sin (i.e., condemnation to hell), nonetheless one's temporal punishments due to sin remain. Why is this? While the sacrament of reconciliation removes eternal punishment through Christ's saving death and resurrection, the penitent needs to satisfy the remaining temporal punishment for sin by performing the penance imposed by the priest, plus doing additional penitential deeds, either in this life or in purgatory. These acts of penance are ways to cleanse us of the stain of guilt, such as described in Psalm 51:2—"Wash me thoroughly from my iniquity, and cleanse me from my sin!"—and 51:7—"Purge me with hyssop, and I shall be clean; wash me, and I shall be whiter than snow."

The great Christian apologist C. S. Lewis, though not a Catholic himself, recognized this truth very well when he wrote that no one would attend a great dinner wearing dirty clothes; one would want to clean up before seeing the king. So also, the temporal punishments due to sin are ways of "cleaning ourselves up" so that we can enter heaven cleansed of our moral imperfections. In fact, the term "purgatory" contains this understanding of purging or cleansing, referring to a moral purification.

**84. Doesn't this idea of the temporal punishment due to sin mean that Jesus' sufferings on the cross were not enough to save us?**

Not at all. The Church teaches that the passion, death, and resurrection of Jesus Christ won redemption for human beings and is the means of the forgiveness of sin (see CCC 613–615). However, the temporal punishment (or chastisement) we suffer for our sins is not due to any inadequacy in Christ's redemption or to the Father's displeasure. Rather, like a true Father, God chastises the children He loves so that we might grow closer to Him: "My son, do not despise the Lord's discipline, nor be weary of his reproof, for the Lord reproves him whom he loves, as a father the son in whom he delights" (Prv 3:11–12).

The lesson found in this quotation from Proverbs is echoed throughout the Old Testament. Here are just a few of the passages:

- "Blessed is the man whom thou dost chasten, O Lord, and whom thou dost teach out of thy law" (Ps 94:12).

- "The Lord has chastened me sorely, but he has not given me over to death" (Ps 118:18).

- "I know, O Lord, that thy judgments are right, and that in faithfulness thou hast afflicted me" (Ps 119:75).

- "Behold, happy is the man whom God reproves; therefore despise not the chastening of the Almighty. For he wounds, but he binds up; he smites, but his hands heal" (Jb 5:17–18).

God uses temporal punishment as a remedy for our sinful actions by turning their painful consequences into means of making us holy. St. Paul, who preached salvation by faith, also taught that "suffering produces endurance, and endurance produces character; and character produces hope, and hope does not disappoint us, because God's love has been poured into our hearts through the Holy Spirit who has been given to us" (Rom 5:3-5).

Therefore, the temporal punishment due to sin is neither a sign of Christ's failure nor an expression of the Father's anger, but is rather a way in which the loving and forgiving God uses the effects of sin to make us thoroughly holy.

### 85.  So all of the temporal punishment due for one's sins must be remitted before one can enter heaven?

Yes. All of the temporary punishment due to sin must be remitted for each and every soul who is saved by Jesus Christ. This punishment is undergone either on earth or in purgatory and has a definite limit set by the wisdom and mercy of God; it is experienced and endures only to the degree necessary for an individual to make satisfaction for the sins he or she has committed (see CCC 1472-1473).

### 86.  OK, so what actually is purgatory?

As the *Catechism* states, "All who die in God's grace and friendship, but still imperfectly purified, are indeed assured of their eternal salvation; but after death they undergo purification, so as to achieve the holiness necessary to enter the joy of heaven" (CCC 1030). Thus, purgatory is a state of existence for redeemed souls who are not yet pure enough to be able to enter heaven.

In the book of Revelation we read that "nothing unclean shall enter [heaven], nor any one who practices abomination or falsehood, but only those who are written in the Lamb's book of life" (Rv 21:27). While the abominations and falsehoods spoken of here refer to those who have sinned mortally and have refused to repent—and thereby bring about their own condemnation to hell—even those who have sincerely repented and been forgiven any mortal sins may still need to make satisfaction for them. God will purify such redeemed souls prior to entering heaven. As St. Paul points out in his first letter to the Corinthians, "If any man's work is burned up, he will suffer loss, though he himself will be saved, but only as through fire" (1 Cor 3:15).

The grace of God won by Christ Jesus and the prayers of the Church, the Body of Christ, can aid the process of purification of the soul. From its very earliest days, the Church has offered prayers for departed souls, including Masses for the repose of a particular deceased soul (see CCC 1032).

In his work *Letters to Malcolm*, C.S. Lewis offers a well-phrased explanation of the need for such a purgatorial state:

> Our souls demand Purgatory, don't they? Would it not break the heart if God said to us, "It is true, my son, that your breath smells and your rags drip with mud and slime, but we are charitable here and no one will upbraid you with these things, nor draw away from you. Enter into the joy"? Should we not reply, "With submission, sir, and if there is no objection, I'd rather be cleansed first." "It may hurt, you know"—"Even so, sir. I assume that the process of purification will normally involve suffering. Partly from tradition; partly because most real good that has been done me in this life involved it. But I don't think suffering is the purpose of the purgation.... The treatment given will be the one required, whether it hurts little or much. (C. S. Lewis, *Letters to Malcolm* [New York: Harcourt Brace Jovanovich, 1963], 108–109).

## 87. Is purgatory found in the Bible?

Though the word *purgatory* is not found in the Bible, the reality of a purification of those who die in God's grace is referred to in a number of biblical passages, including 2 Maccabees 12:45, 1 Corinthians 3:15, and 1 Peter 1:7. (By the way, a number of fundamental theological terms accepted by the majority of Christians are not explicitly found in the Bible, e.g., Trinity, Incarnation, etc., but the truths that these terms describe most certainly are found there.)

The first thing to note is that the New Testament speaks of a prison for souls that is neither heaven nor hell. We read in 1 Peter 3:18-20, that "Christ also died for sins once for all, the righteous for the unrighteous, that he might bring us to God, being put to death in the flesh but made alive in the spirit; in which he went and preached to the spirits in prison, who formerly did not obey."

Christ was able to preach to those souls who had died before his redemptive death, and this preaching was able to take them from this "prison" into heaven. A passage from the gospel of Matthew illuminates this text further: "Make friends quickly with your accuser, while you are going with him to court, lest your accuser hand you over to the judge, and the judge to the guard, and you be put in prison; truly, I say to you, you will never get out till you have paid the last penny" (Mt 5:25-26). This passage explicitly mentions remaining in this prison for a time, a time limited by "paying the last penny" of some debt that is to be exacted by the "judge." Further support occurs in Matthew 12:32:

"And whoever says a word against the Son of man will be forgiven; but whoever speaks against the Holy Spirit will not be forgiven, either in this age or in the age to come." This text, like 5:26, assumes that one can be forgiven in the "age to come," that is, after death.

St. Paul also speaks of the testing of one's work for the Lord:

> For no other foundation can any one lay than that which is laid, which is Jesus Christ. Now if any one builds on the foundation with gold, silver, precious stones, wood, hay, straw—each man's work will become manifest; for the Day will disclose it, because it will be revealed with fire, and the fire will test what sort of work each one has done. If the work which any man has built on the foundation survives, he will receive a reward. If any man's work is burned up, he will suffer loss, though he himself will be saved, but only as through fire (1 Cor 3:11-15).

The purifying fire that tests one's Christian effort is a preparation for the Day of the Lord and heaven. Note, though, that the man is certain of being saved, even if he suffers some loss through the purifying fire. This text definitely pertains to the Church's teaching on purgatory.

**88. Where in Scripture can we find the idea that people on earth can help souls in purgatory through their prayers and sacrifices?**

The first indication of our ability to help the souls in purgatory comes from the Old Testament, in the second book of Maccabees:

Then under the tunic of every one of the dead they found sacred tokens of the idols of Jamnia, which the law forbids the Jews to wear. And it became clear to all that this was why these men had fallen. So they all blessed the ways of the Lord, the righteous Judge, who reveals the things that are hidden; and they turned to prayer, beseeching that the sin which had been committed might be wholly blotted out. And the noble Judas exhorted the people to keep themselves free from sin, for they had seen with their own eyes what had happened because of the sin of those who had fallen. He also took up a collection, man by man, to the amount of two thousand drachmas of silver, and sent it to Jerusalem to provide for a sin offering. In doing this he acted very well and honorably, taking account of the resurrection. For if he were not expecting that those who had fallen would rise again, it would have been superfluous and foolish to pray for the dead. But if he was looking to the splendid reward that is laid up for those who fall asleep in godliness, it was a holy and pious thought. Therefore he made atonement for the dead, that they might be delivered from their sin (2 Mc 12:40-45).

Judas Maccabeus understood that a sacrifice could be offered to help the souls of otherwise good men who had sinned. This would help them attain resurrection from the dead. The early Christians continued this practice of praying for the dead on the anniversary of their death. St. Perpetua, for example, prayed for the soul of her young brother just before she was martyred, and St. Monica asked her son, St. Augustine, to pray for her soul after she died. The inscriptions on many early Christian tombs make similar requests.

## 89. What is an indulgence?

The *Catechism* identifies an indulgence as a merit "obtained through the Church" to help individual Christians by opening the treasury of Christ's merits and the merits of the saints "to obtain from the Father of mercies the remission of the temporal punishment due for their sins" (CCC 1478). An indulgence is either *partial* or *plenary* (i.e., "full"), depending upon whether it removes part or all of the punishment due to sin (see CCC 1471).

The Church can offer indulgences by virtue of Christ's gift of the power "bind and loose" (see Mt 16:19, 18:18; CCC 1478) —that is, in addition to the authority to forgive sin, it has the power to remove ("to loose") the temporal punishment due to sin. The Church gives these indulgences not only to help Christians be free of the temporal punishment they deserve, but also to inspire them to do works of devotion, penance, and charity. Thus, Christians can perform various works and say prayers which gain indulgences for themselves or for others.

Pope Paul VI, in his 1967 apostolic constitution on indulgences, *Indulgentiarum doctrina*, clarified two important points: 1) an indulgence remits "the temporal punishment due to sins whose guilt has already been forgiven." This presupposes that the person has already repented and confessed the sins for which an indulgence is being sought; and 2) "the faithful Christian who is duly disposed gains [an indulgence] under certain defined conditions through the Church's help." The proper disposition is one of faith in Christ, and the right "conditions" refer to the person being in a state of grace, usually associated with receiving the sacraments of reconciliation and holy communion, and praying for the intentions of the pope.

## 90. Does the Bible teach anything about indulgences?

As with question eighty-seven on purgatory, the answer to this question is found in 2 Maccabees 12:42, where Judas Maccabeus told his soldiers to pray "that the sin which had been committed [by the dead soldiers] might be wholly blotted out."

As we have mentioned previously, the authority of the Church to grant indulgences comes with the power granted by Jesus when He told Peter, "I will give you the keys of the kingdom of heaven, and whatever you bind on earth shall be bound in heaven, and whatever you loose on earth shall be loosed in heaven" (Mt 16:19). He reiterated this same teaching later when He said to the apostles as a whole, "Truly, I say to you, whatever you bind on earth shall be bound in heaven, and whatever you loose on earth shall be loosed in heaven" (Mt 18:18; see CCC 1478).

Another key idea underlying indulgences is that the Church has a "treasury of merit" available to distribute to her members (see CCC 1476–1477). Two passages traditionally understood as referring to this profound truth both come from St. Paul's letter to the Ephesians: "Blessed be the God and Father of our Lord Jesus Christ, who has blessed us in Christ with every spiritual blessing in the heavenly places, even as he chose us in him before the foundation of the world, that we should be holy and blameless before him" (Eph 1:3-4). This first passage emphasizes that God has blessed us—i.e., the Church—with every spiritual blessing. God is the origin and source of these blessings, but He has given them to us so that all members of the Church might be "holy and blameless," that is, pure and clean in order to enter heaven. Remember, nothing unclean can enter there (see Rv 21:27). These blessings make it possible for members of the Church to become blameless and eligible for heaven.

The second text mentions the Church's disposition of these blessings: "For this reason I, Paul, a prisoner for Christ Jesus on behalf of you Gentiles, assuming that you have heard of the stewardship of God's grace that was given to me for you..." (Eph 3:1-2). We can see, then, that St. Paul, as an apostle, is a steward of the grace of God's grace. God is the source the grace, but He has given stewardship over His grace to the apostles (see Mt 18:18). This means that the Church has the authority and power to distribute God's grace as a good steward distributes his master's goods.

## 91. Did the early Church believe in indulgences?

Yes, and we can see that the apostolic Church understood the notion of merit from the words of Christ in Matthew 6:1-6:

> Beware of practicing your piety before men in order to be seen by them; for then you will have no reward from your Father who is in heaven ... when you give alms do not let your left hand know what your right hand is doing, so that your alms may be in secret; and your

Father who sees in secret will reward you ... when you pray, go into your room and shut the door and pray to your Father who is in secret; and your Father who sees in secret will reward you.

The practice of applying the merits of the saints to others appeared during the age of martyrdom. Those Christians who witnessed the martyrdom of their fellow believers would cry out petitions to them before they died. It came to be seen that the martyrs, by shedding their blood for the witness of Christ and the Gospel, gained them direct entrance to heaven (i.e., without the need for purification in purgatory). Thus, they would be able to present the petitions of the Church on earth directly to God. We can see this reflected in the book of Revelation: "And the twenty-four elders fell down before the Lamb, each holding a harp, and with golden bowls full of incense, which are the prayers of the saints" (Rv 5:8). Therefore, Christians sought the intercession of the saints even at the moment of their martyrdom. The belief was that these martyrs' prayers and merits, won by dying for Jesus Christ, would mitigate their own temporal punishment and penance due to their sins.

Tertullian, the great third-century apologist, wrote that Christians appealed to martyrs to intervene for them: "Some, not able to find this peace in the Church, have been used to seek it from the imprisoned martyrs" (*Ad Martyras*, I). Later, St. Augustine would be asked by his dying mother, St. Monica, to remember her at Mass, praying for her soul (see *Confessions*, Book IX, 10-11). These are just a few examples of early Christians showing their faith that other Christians could do good for their souls by the merits they had won and then applied to other persons.

## 92. Are Catholics still required to believe in indulgences?

Yes. Indulgences are part of the dogmatic teaching of the Church. This means that no Catholic is at liberty to ignore or disbelieve in them. In 1415, the Council of Constance affirmed the use of indulgences, and the Council of Trent in 1563, in reaction to the opposition of Martin Luther and other Protestant "reformers" to indulgences, definitively stated that "[this] holy council teaches and commands that the use of indulgences, most salutary to the Christian people and approved by the authority of the holy councils, is to be retained in the Church, and it condemns with anathema those who assert that they are useless or deny that there is in the Church the power of granting them" (Council of Trent, Session XXV, December 4, 1563). This dogma on indulgences was reaffirmed in Pope Paul VI's 1967 apostolic constitution *Indulgentiarum doctrina* and in the *Catechism of the Catholic Church,* issued in 1994 (see CCC 1471–1479).

## 93. Is there a basis in Scripture to believe that one person's merits can benefit another person?

Yes, both the Old and New Testaments present certain people whose merits benefited others. For example, Abraham believed God, who then counted this faith as righteousness (Gn 15:6). God not only favored Abraham but also extended His favor to Abraham's descendants, who would be as numerous as the stars or the sand along the sea (15:5). They are beneficiaries of God's promise because of Abraham's faith. St. Paul takes up the same theme in Romans 11:28–29, stating that God loves the Jews because of their ancestors: "As regards election they are beloved for the sake of their forefathers. For the gifts and the call of God are irrevocable."

Another example concerns Solomon, who deserved punishment for allowing his foreign wives to build temples to their deities:

> [T]he Lord said to Solomon: "Since this is what you want, and you have not kept my covenant and my statutes which I enjoined on you, I will deprive you of the kingdom and give it to your servant. I will not do this during your lifetime, however, for the sake of your father David; it is your son whom I will deprive. Nor will I take away the whole kingdom. I will leave your son one tribe for the sake of my servant David and of Jerusalem, which I have chosen" (1 Kgs 11:11–13)

However, God does not punish Solomon because of the merits and love of his father, David. David's goodness was able to protect Solomon from God's wrath. Note, however, that Solomon's son Rehoboam chose to act foolishly and cruelly to the people of the ten northern tribes. As a result, they revolted against him and the kingdom split in two (see 1 Kings 12:13–16). He was not able to benefit from merits pertaining to his father, Solomon, since the latter was already drawing upon those of his predecessor, David.

**94. Can the souls in purgatory pray for themselves in order to speed up their entry into heaven?**

No. Souls in purgatory are not able to pray for or help themselves in any way. In purgatory, souls can only receive benefits passively, simply by undergoing the suffering necessary and by receiving the prayers, sacrifices, fasting, and good works of people on earth. The suffering souls are completely dependent on the charity of others: on Christ's love for them and on the love of others who remember them in their prayers and sacrifices.

**95. I have seen some older prayers which promise hundred or even thousands of days indulgence. How did the Church determine the number of days indulgence that a particular prayer is worth?**

Prior to the reforms following the Second Vatican Council, the Church typically defined a certain number of days (or even years) indulgence for certain prayers or actions. This practice of assigning specific time designations does not come from a Catholic belief in some kind of a "purgatorial clock." In fact, since purgatory is a spiritual state outside of earthly time and space, there can be no designation of days or years there. Rather, the designation of a certain number of days (or years) indulgence was meant to indicate the equivalent number of days of penance that would have been accomplished by those prayers or acts during life on earth. Remember, penance in the early centuries of the Church was public (as private confession did not become the norm until the seventh century), and a person could receive a penance lasting twenty years before they were granted absolution. The days of indulgence reduced the period of such long penances. In other words, certain prayers were said to have the same benefit as a year of penance on bread and water.

However, in order to avoid any confusion that the period of indulgence meant a reduction of time in purgatory, Pope Paul VI in 1967 discontinued the custom of numbering the days and years of indulgences (see *Indulgentiarum doctrina*). In its place, he simply identified some indulgences as *plenary* (or complete), indicating that these remove all temporal punishment due to sin, and others as *partial*, whereby some temporal punishment remains. He further stated that

> the faithful can obtain, in addition to the merit which is the principal fruit of the act, a further remission of temporal punishment in proportion to the degree to which the charity of the one performing the act is greater, and in proportion to the degree to which the act itself is performed in a more perfect way (*Indulgentiarum doctrina*, 12).

Thus we can see that charity is the key to understanding and obtaining indulgences. They should not be viewed as some sort of magical powers under the control of human whims. The grace of God, which empowers us to love others for their own sake, is the fundamental element in seeking God's mercy for the souls in purgatory.

## 96. Don't indulgences duplicate—or even negate—the salvific work of Christ?

Not at all. First, the mission and work of Christ was to save humanity from eternal condemnation in hell and open the gates of eternal life; to accomplish this, He suffered, died, and rose from the dead. Indulgences in no way add to or negate this fundamental work of our salvation. Indulgences are not an alternative to redemption in Christ, but rather a consequence of it. Those who are still living in sin must turn to Christ in faith, repent of their sins, and trust in His mercy. In addition, all indulgences granted by the Church deal only with the temporal punishment due to sin, and they derive all their power from the Church's treasury of merit. The basis of this whole treasury is the infinite merit of Jesus Christ. Even the merit gained by the saints can benefit others only because the saints are united to Jesus as their Head. Thus, the merit won by Christians on earth is effective only because they are doing God's will in union with Christ.

Based on these principles, then, indulgences neither duplicate not replace the infinite merits of Jesus Christ. Indulgences depend on His merit and apply them to souls in need of the remission of temporal punishment due to sin, according to the authority "to bind and loose" Jesus gave to the Church (see Mt 16:19, 18:18).

## 97. How does a person gain an indulgence?

The answer to this can be found in the *Enchiridion of Indulgences*, issued in 1968. Paragraph 22 lists the requirements for gaining an indulgence: one must be baptized, in the state of grace (at least at the completion of the works prescribed for receiving the particular indulgence), in full communion with the Church (i.e., not excommunicated), and a subject of the one granting the indulgence. The person granting the indulgence is usually the pope, so those indulgences apply to every Catholic subject to him. However, sometimes an indulgence is granted by a bishop. To receive such an indulgence one must be a subject of that particular prelate.

If one meets the above criteria, he or she is eligible to receive an indulgence. However, in addition to these qualifications, the person must have at least a general intention to gain the indulgence. In other words, one cannot receive an indulgence unintentionally or by accident. Furthermore, the person must perform the works enjoined by the indulgence at the time and in the manner prescribed by it. Such works are specified in the description of the indulgence.

## 98. What's the difference between a plenary and a partial indulgence?

A plenary indulgence removes all of the temporal punishment due to sin. A partial indulgence removes only part of the temporal punishment, though, as Pope Paul VI teaches in *Indulgentiarum doctrina* (January 1,

1967), the Church does not specify the quantity of a partial indulgence. In either case, an indulgence can remove only the temporal punishment which is due to sins committed up to that point in time; indulgences cannot be applied to the temporal punishments due to sin in the future.

## 99. What must one do to gain a plenary or complete indulgence?

Again, the *Enchiridion of Indulgences* (1968), paragraph 24, authoritatively explains what one must do to gain a plenary indulgence. Any person can gain one plenary indulgence on a given day, but not more than that, except on All Souls' Day, a day dedicated to praying for the souls in purgatory. On that day one can gain up to three plenary indulgences. Also, a person can receive a plenary indulgence at the moment of death, even if he or she had received another plenary indulgence on the same day.

Paragraph 26 of the *Enchiridion* further specifies the need to perform not only the work to which the indulgence is attached but also to fulfill the following three conditions: 1) make a sacramental confession; 2) receive holy communion; and 3) pray for the intentions of the pope, usually an Our Father and a Hail Mary at minimum, though other prayers for his intentions may be added (paragraph 29). These three conditions can be fulfilled several days before or after the performance of the work prescribed for the indulgence, though it is fitting that holy communion be received and the prayer for the intention of the Sovereign Pontiff be prayed on the same day the work is performed (paragraph 27). A single sacramental confession suffices for gaining several plenary indulgences over a period of days (remember, one may receive only one plenary indulgence in a day). However, communion must be received and the prayer for the intention of the pope must be recited for the gaining of each plenary indulgence.

Finally, the Church requires that the person seeking the indulgence have no attachment to sin, even venial sin, which means that the person must renounce sin and truly desire never to commit sin again. Such an interior disposition indicates the true repentance that makes the indulgence worthwhile. If the latter disposition is in any way less than perfect or if the prescribed three conditions are not fulfilled, the indulgence will be partial only (paragraph 26).

### 100. How does one gain a partial indulgence?

Simply, one must perform the actions or say the prayers required in order to obtain the indulgence. However, to gain a partial indulgence, one does not need to receive confession and holy communion, nor is it necessary to say the prayers for the intentions of the pope (though this would always be a good thing to do). Neither is it necessary for one to have a complete detachment from sin, as is required for a plenary indulgence. While these points indicate that a lesser degree of sanctity still allow one to be a candidate to receive a partial indulgence, they also show that a greater degree of holiness makes a partial indulgence more effective. In fact, one's interior disposition to holiness and union with Christ affect the ability of a person to be receptive to the merciful indulgences God wants to grant for the remission of the temporal punishment due to sin.

## 101. I've heard that the Divine Mercy devotion can atone for one's sins.

Yes, a plenary indulgence is granted for Divine Mercy Sunday, which is the first Sunday after Easter. As with all plenary indulgences, the person must be free from attachment to sin (even venial sin), be in the state of grace, and go to confession and receive holy communion within a few days before or after Divine Mercy Sunday (usually a week or ten days before or after the feast). There are a number of ways to gain the indulgence. One is to take part in the prayers and devotions held in honor of the Divine Mercy in any church or chapel. A second way is to recite the Our Father and the Creed, adding a devout prayer to the merciful Lord Jesus (e.g. "Merciful Jesus, I trust in you!") in the presence of the Blessed Sacrament, whether the Eucharist is exposed or remains reserved in the tabernacle.

One can gain a partial indulgence by praying an approved invocation to the merciful Lord Jesus (e.g., "Jesus, I trust in You," "My Jesus, mercy," etc.) with a contrite heart.

A person who cannot go to church due to serious illness can still receive a plenary indulgence by totally detesting sin, having the intention of fulfilling as soon as possible the three usual conditions of confession, holy communion, and prayers for the Holy Father, and reciting the Our Father and the Apostles' Creed before a devout image of Our Merciful Lord Jesus. One can also pray a devout invocation to the Merciful Lord Jesus (e.g., "Merciful Jesus, I trust in you").

If even these actions are truly impossible, then one can unite oneself spiritually with those carrying out the prescribed practice for obtaining the indulgence in the usual way and offer to the Merciful Lord a prayer and the sufferings of their illness and the difficulties of their lives. They should resolve to accomplish the three conditions prescribed to obtain the plenary indulgence as soon as possible.

# Preparing to Celebrate the Sacrament of Reconciliation

## INTRODUCTION

When preparing to make a good confession, it is a good idea to spend some time beforehand meditating on your recent transgressions in an "examination of conscience." Such an examination should help you to better recognize and develop a stronger awareness of how you have offended the Lord.

The following reflections are not comprehensive, but they cover some of the most commonly-committed sins. When reflecting on your sins, it would be a mistake to approach your offenses with a legalistic mind set. That is, do not approach your sin as though you are merely reviewing violations of an arbitrary code of rules. The essence of sin is pride, and therefore you would do well to examine those instances in which your own self-interest superseded the will of God, to the detriment of everyone affected by your decisions and possibly with eternal consequences for you.

In addition to being necessary for our salvation, the Ten Commandments provide a helpful model for reflecting on our sins. They are given in Exodus 20:1-17 and Deuteronomy 5:6-21, with the shorter version in Deuteronomy being the more familiar of the two. Other references to parallel teachings of Jesus Christ are also cited here. You may also find it helpful to examine your sins while praying or meditating on the passages of the Bible found here. This will help you to see sin not as the violation of arbitrary rules imposed by human beings but as a violation of the express will of God, as revealed in the Scriptures and taught by Our Lord Jesus Christ.

## An Examination of Conscience

### BASED ON THE TEN COMMANDMENTS

1. **I am the Lord your God. You shall have no other gods before Me.** (see Mt 4:10, 22:36-38; Mk 7:14-23)

   - Have I doubted or denied the existence of God?
   - Have I lost hope of salvation or despaired of God's mercy?
   - Have I refused to believe those things God has revealed in Scripture and Tradition?
   - Have I engaged or believed in fortune telling, horoscopes, the occult, good-luck charms, tarot cards, palmistry, Ouija boards, séances, or reincarnation?
   - Have I denied or refused to defend my Catholic Faith?
   - Have I spent time in prayer on a daily basis?
   - Have I ever received Communion in a state of mortal sin?
   - Have I ever deliberately told a lie in confession or have I withheld a mortal sin from the priest in confession?
   - Am I addicted to any sort of chemical substance or self-indulgent behavior that alters my ability to be a "free-thinking" and "free-choosing" individual?
   - Have I let hobbies or forms of leisure and

entertainment become the most important aspects of my life?

- Are my ultimate highs and lows in life based on following sports entertainment?

2. **You shall not take the name of the Lord your God in vain.** (see Mt 5:33-37, 22:36-38; Acts 19:13-17; Col 3:17)

- Have I blasphemed or insulted God?
- Have I used God's name in vain, that is, in a careless or frivolous manner?
- Have I cursed someone by wishing evil upon them?
- Have I broken an oath or a vow, such as perjuring myself in a legal trial?
- Have I gotten angry at God?
- Have I insulted a sacred person or abused a sacred object?
- Do I hesitate to mention God's name in appropriate situations, in conversations with friends and family members, such as social and political discussions which have a religious dimension to them?
- Have I neglected learning more about God through study and reflection?

3. **Keep the Sabbath day holy.** (see Mt 22:36-38; Mk 2:27-28; Heb 4:9)

- Do I  attend Mass every Sunday?
- Have I missed attending Mass on any holy day of obligation?
- Do I arrive at Mass on time? Do I leave early?
- When I participate in the Mass, do I focus on

the liturgy and my prayers, or do I let my mind wander and dwell on unrelated subjects?

- Do choose to work on Sundays when I am not obligated to?
- Do I disregard the religious observance of the Sabbath in general?

4. **Honor your Father and Mother.** (see Mt 15:4-6, 19:19, 22:39-40; Rom 13:9; 1 Cor 4:14-17; Eph 6:1-3)

- Have I disobeyed authority, be it that of my parents, employer, government laws, or Church teaching?
- Did I neglect my duties to my husband, wife, children, or parents?
- Did I neglect to give good religious example to my family?
- Did I fail to actively take an interest in the religious education and moral formation of my children?
- Do I set legitimate moral norms for my children and do I enforce the consequences of bad behavior?
- Have I caused tension and fights in my family?
- Have I cared for my aged and infirm relatives?
- Have I disrespected or belittled the elderly?

5. **You shall not kill.** (see Mt 19:18, 22:39-40; Rom 13:9; Eph 4:31)

- Have I killed or physically injured anyone?
- Have I had an abortion, or have I encouraged or assisted someone else to get one? Have I attempted to commit suicide?

- Do I support the right to suicide?
- Did I use or cause my spouse to use birth control pills (whether or not realizing that birth control pills do abort the fetus if and when conceived)?
- Have I taken part in or given my approval to a "mercy killing" (euthanasia)?
- Did I become angry, impatient, envious, unkind, proud, vengeful, jealous, or hateful toward another?
- Have I engaged in unjustifiable physical violence toward others?
- Have I abused my children by violent or other means?

6.  **You shall not commit adultery.** (see Mt 19:18, 22:39-40; Mk 7:22; Rom 13:9; Eph 5:3-4).

- Do I look at pornography or read romance novels for the purpose of enhancing my own self-indulgent fantasies?
- Did I use impure or suggestive words? Tell impure stories? Listen to them?
- Did I commit impure acts by myself (masturbation)?
- Did I commit impure acts with another, whether fornication (premarital sex) or adultery (sex with a married person)?
- Have I engaged in homosexual activity?
- Do I treat my own spouse as an object of my personal sexual gratification?
- Have I practiced artificial birth control (by any means, including pills, devices, withdrawal)?
- Have I or has my spouse voluntarily been sterilized?

- Have I sought a divorce or encouraged others to do so without a grave reason (e.g., concern for violence)?
- Did I marry or advise anyone to marry outside the Church?

7. **You shall not steal.** (see Mt 19:18, 22:39-40; Mk 7:21; Rom 13:9; Eph 4:28)

- Have I stolen other people's property?
- Have I helped or encouraged others to steal or keep stolen goods?
- Have I knowingly bought or kept goods that I knew were stolen by someone else?
- Have I made restitution for any goods that I have stolen or returned goods that I knew were stolen by another?
- Have I failed to keep any contracts I have entered?
- When making a purchase, have I remained silent when recognizing a monetary mistake in my favor?
- Have I given or accepted bribes or kickbacks, especially to increase my influence in government or business matters?
- Have I paid my bills responsibly?
- Have I incurred unnecessary debt?
- Have I gambled money in such a way as to deprive myself or my family of the necessities of life?
- Have I neglected my duties while on the clock, failing to put in an honest day's work for the wages that I earn?
- Have I abused my work time by using it for personal interests, such as focusing on social communications via e-mail or phone calls when I should have been working?

- Do I pay my employees a fair wage by which they are able to adequately support themselves and their families?
- Do I take advantage of the religious beliefs of my employees by telling them that their work is a ministry, so as to justify the low wages I pay them, when I could easily pay them more?
- Do I share my goods with the poor and needy, showing generosity to them?

8. **You shall not bear false witness against your neighbor.** (see Mt 5:33, 19:18, 22:39-40; Rom 13:9; Eph 4:25)

- Have I told any lies?
- Have I deliberately deceived any persons who had the right to know the truth of a matter?
- Have I injured the reputation or effectiveness of other persons by spreading falsehoods about them?
- Have I given a false testimony in court or in a legal procedure, thereby committing perjury?
- Do I deal with other persons in a sincere and honest manner?
- Did I fail to keep secret what I should have kept confidential?
- Have I gossiped about friends or enemies, revealing personal private information that is detrimental in nature? Have I done so without even knowing with certainty the truth of the matter?
- Do I criticize others or hold negative and uncharitable thoughts about them?
- Has my reluctance to speak in defense of truth or the faith because of my own fear or laziness led others to sin, or made them susceptible to it?

- Has my own taste for immoral actions or events encouraged others to follow suit and deny God's will?

9. **You shall not covet your neighbor's wife.** (see Mt 5:27-28, 19:18, 22:39-40; Rom 13:9; Eph 5:3-4).

- Since this commandment treats the issues of one's interior desires rather than overtly sinful deeds, one must examine mental attitudes and choices one makes about thoughts one dwells on.
- Did I respect all members of the opposite sex, or have I thought of other people as objects?
- Have there been times in which I chose to dwell on lust, even if I have not acted on it?
- Have I reflected on past sexual sins for the purpose of indulging in the reminiscence of the gratification those recollections offer?
- Have I instigated or actively engaged in impure thoughts by reading books, seeing movies, or listening to conversations which are sexually stimulating?
- Do I try to steer my imagination from lustful thoughts that treat other persons as objects for my use rather than as objects of pure love?
- Do I pray when I am tempted by impure thoughts? Do I direct my thoughts to other things so as to resist the temptation to lust?

10. **You shall not covet your neighbor's goods.** (see Mt 6:21, 19:18; Mk 7:22)

- This commandment also concerns internal attitudes rather than overt actions, though here it concerns the neighbor's property.
- Have I envied other people's families or possessions?
- Have I made it a primary goal in life to acquire as many material possessions as possible?
- Have I felt compelled to 'keep up with the Jones"?
- Do I always want more than I have?
- Do I always like to upgrade to the latest car, latest model electronic appliances and equipment, even when I do not need such upgrades?
- Am I greedy or selfish in regard to my possessions?
- Do I place my trust in God's providence, entrusting my material and spiritual needs to His care?
- Do we thank God for all He has given us and are we satisfied with these gifts?

# Celebrating the Sacrament of Reconciliation

In the previous pages, we considered how one should properly prepare for confession. We will now describe how the sacrament of reconciliation is actually celebrated in the Roman rite of the Church. According to the official Rite of Penance, issued in 1973, the sacrament contains the following components:

## 1. Preparation

As we have previously described, prior to actually going to confession, the penitent examines his or her conscience, using the Ten Commandments, the Beatitudes, or the example of Christ as a guide to measure his or her thoughts, words, actions, or omissions.

## 2. Entering the Confessional or Reconciliation Room

The priest and the penitent both make the sign of the cross, "In the name of the Father, and of the Son, and of the Holy Spirit. Amen." The priest then invites the penitent to trust in God's mercy and confidently confess his or her sins.

Traditionally, the penitent asks for the priest's blessing with the words, "Bless me, Father, for I have sinned. It has been [*x* weeks/months/years] since my last confession." It is also appropriate for the penitent to tell the priest his or her state of life, i.e., married, single, or religious.

## 3. The Scriptural Reading

At this point, according to the revised rite of 1973, the priest has the option of reading a short passage from Scripture. In the interest of time, however, this is often omitted.

## 4. The Confession of One's Sins

The penitent then confesses his or her sins, indicating the number of times one has committed a particular sin (especially if it is a serious sin) to the best of his or her recollection. During the confession of sins, the priest may interject with clarifying questions or to offer guidance and encouragement. It is important for the priest to have a true understanding of the circumstances surrounding certain sins in order to provide the best counsel and impose the proper penance.

According to the *Catechism of the Catholic Church*, it is by the actual confession of one's sins that a penitent "looks squarely at the sins he is guilty of, takes responsibility for them, and thereby opens himself again to God and to the communion of the Church in order to make a new future possible" (see CCC 1455).

When one has finished confessing his or her sins, the priest offers appropriate advice to help the penitent gain an understanding of their sins and how to avoid occasions of sin in the future. If necessary, the priest may also encourage the penitent to make restitution for the harm he or she has caused others. He then imposes an act of penance or satisfaction appropriate to the seriousness of the sins confessed. Examples of typical penances would include certain prayers (e.g., "pray three Our Fathers and three Hail Marys"), an act of self-denial, or and act of charity (e.g., performing a corporal or spiritual work of mercy).

## 5. The Act of Contrition

At this point, the priest asks the penitent to pray an act of contrition, a prayer which expresses sorrow for one's sins and a resolution not to sin (and to avoid occasions of sin) in the future. Typically, confessionals and reconciliation rooms provide a card with several forms of the act of contrition. The penitent may also recite it from memory.

Here is the traditional form of the act of contrition:

> O my God, I am heartily sorry for having offended Thee, and I detest all my sins because I dread the loss of heaven and the pains of hell; but most of all because they offend Thee, my God, Who are all-good and deserving of all my love. I firmly resolve, with the help of Thy grace, to confess my sins, to do penance, and to amend my life. Amen.

## 6. Absolution by the Priest

Following the act of contrition, the priest extends his right hand (or both hands) over the head of the penitent and pronounces the words of absolution. This constitutes the "form" of the sacrament of penance (whereas the actual confession of sins is the "matter.") One's sins are actually forgiven when the priest pronounces the words "I absolve you of your sins in the name of the Father, and of the Son, and of the Holy Spirit."

God, the Father of mercies, through the death and resurrection of his Son has reconciled the world to himself
and sent the Holy Spirit among us for the forgiveness of
sins; through the ministry of the Church may God give
you pardon and peace, and I absolve you from your sins
in the name of the Father, and of the Son, and of the Holy
Spirit. Amen.

The penitent answers, "Amen."

## 7. Dismissal of the Penitent

The priest then dismisses the penitent, with the words
"The Lord has freed you from your sins, go in peace." The
penitent strives to be ever more converted to the Gospel,
expressing this commitment by a life renewed by God's
grace.

# Glossary of Terms

The following glossary seeks to present the teachings of the *Catechism of the Catholic Church* on the various aspects of confession and related issues.

**Absolution, words of:** the sacramental formula pronounced by the priest through which "God grants the penitent 'pardon and peace,'" from their sins (CCC 1424).

**Adultery:** "marital infidelity" (CCC 2380).

**Age of reason (discretion):** in the context of the sacrament of penance, the age at which "each of the faithful is bound by an obligation faithfully to confess serious sins at least once a year" (CCC 1457; see also CIC 989).

**Apostasy:** "the total [post-baptismal] repudiation of the Christian faith" (CCC 2089).

**Apostles:** those to whom Christ entrusted "the ministry of reconciliation, bishops who are their successors, and priests, the bishops' collaborators, continue to exercise this ministry" (CCC 1461).

**Attrition:** see *Contrition, Imperfect*

**"Bind and loose":** A reference to Matthew 16:19 (see also Mt 18:18 and 28:16-20) in which "the office of binding and loosing which was given to Peter was also assigned to the college of the apostles united to its head. The words bind and loose mean: whomever you exclude from your communion, will be excluded from communion with God; whomever you receive anew into your communion, God will welcome back into his [communion]" (CCC 1444–1445).

**Blasphemy:** "uttering against God—inwardly or outwardly—words of hatred, reproach, or defiance; in speaking ill of God; in failing in respect toward him in one's speech; in misusing God's name" (CCC 2148).

**Charity:** "The theological virtue by which we love God above all things for his own sake, and our neighbor as ourselves for the love of God" (CCC 1822). This is the "vital principle" in the heart of man; "the source of the good and pure works, which sin wounds," and "mortal sin destroys" (CCC 1853, 1855, 1856).

**Condemnation:** "God predestines no one to go to hell; for this, a willful turning away from God (a mortal sin) is necessary, and persistence in it until the end" (CCC 1037).

**Confession:** a commonly-used name for the sacrament of penance and reconciliation (see CCC 1424); also, the disclosure of sins, "an essential part of the sacrament of Penance: All mortal sins of which penitents after a diligent self-examination are conscious must be recounted by them in confession" (CCC 1456).

**Confessor:** term given to a priest when he is celebrating the sacrament of penance (see CCC 1461).

**Contrition:** in general, the "sorrow of the soul and detestation for the sin committed, together with the resolution not to sin again" (CCC 1451).

**Contrition, imperfect:** is rooted in "the consideration of sin's ugliness or the fear of eternal damnation and the other penalties threatening the sinner (contrition of fear). Such a stirring of conscience can initiate an interior process which, under the prompting of grace, will be brought to completion by sacramental absolution. By itself, however, imperfect contrition cannot obtain the forgiveness of grave sins" (CCC 1454).

**Contrition, perfect:** "arises from a love by which God is loved above all else... Such contrition remits venial sins; it also obtains forgiveness of mortal sins if it includes the firm resolution to have recourse to sacramental confession as soon as possible" (CCC 1452).

**Culpability:** refers to one's "responsibility for an action"; this "can be diminished or even nullified by ignorance, aniadvertence, duress, fear, habit, inordinate attachments, and other psychological or social factors" (CCC 1735).

**Despair:** the vice whereby a person "ceases to hope for his personal salvation from God, for help in attaining it or for the forgiveness of his sins" (CCC 2091).

**Divine law:** is defined as the "eternal law—the source, in God, of all law" (CCC 1952).

**Easter duty:** the second precept of the Church which asks the faithful to confess their sins at least once a year (see CCC 2042).

**Efficacious:** refers to the power of the sacraments to "confer the grace that they signify. They are efficacious because in them Christ himself is at work" (CCC 1127).

**Examination of conscience:** a necessary part of a penitent's preparation for receiving the sacrament of penance; essentially a reflection on the sins one has committed since his or her last confession (see CCC 1454, 1456-1457).

**Excommunication:** "the most severe ecclesiastical penalty, which impedes the reception of the sacraments and the exercise of certain ecclesiastical acts, and for which absolution consequently cannot be granted, according to canon law, except by the Pope, the bishop of the place, or priests authorized by them" (CCC 1463).

**Faculty:** in sacramental theology, this term refers to the delegated ecclesiastical authority a priest receives from the local bishop to hear confessions in a given diocese (see CCC 1462, 1463).

**Final impenitence:** persistence in mortal sin until death (see CCC 1037).

**Firm resolution:** part of contrition, the intention of a penitent to sin no more and avoid occasions of sin (see CCC 1451).

**Form:** in sacramnetial theology, the words and actions required in a particular sacrament for its valid celebration; e.g., in the sacrament of penance, the form is the words of absolution pronounced by the priest at the conclusion of the sacrament.

**Fornication:** "carnal union between an unmarried man and an unmarried woman. It is gravely contrary to the dignity of persons and of human sexuality which is naturally ordered to the good of spouses and the generation and education of children" (CCC 2353)

**Free will:** "the power, rooted in reason and will, to act or not to act, to do this or that, and so to perform deliberate actions on one's own responsibility. By free will one shapes one's own life" (CCC 1731)

**Grace:** "the free and undeserved help that God gives us to respond to his call to become children of God, adoptive sons, partakers of the divine nature and of eternal life. Grace is a participation in the life of God" (CCC 1996–1997).

**Grace, actual:** "God's interventions, whether at the beginning of conversion or in the course of the work of sanctification" (CCC 2000).

**Grace, sanctifying:** "an habitual gift, a stable and supernatural disposition that perfects the soul itself to enable it to live with God, to act by his love" (CCC 2000).

**Grave matter:** an objectively disordered act; "specified by the Ten Commandments" (CCC 1858).

**Grave sin,** see *Sin, mortal.*

**Guilt,** see *Culpability.*

**Habitual sin:** a vice or an addiction; may limit (or remove) one's culpability of a particular sin.

**Hell:** the "state of definitive self-exclusion from communion with God and the blessed... Immediately after death the souls of those who die in a state of mortal sin descend into hell, where they suffer the punishments of hell, 'eternal fire.' The chief punishment of hell is eternal separation from God, in whom alone man can possess the life and happiness for which he was created and for which he longs" (CCC 1033, 1035).

**Heresy:** "the obstinate post-baptismal denial of some truth which must be believed with divine and Catholic faith, or it is likewise an obstinate doubt concerning the same" (CCC 2089).

**Indulgence:** is defined as "a remission before God of the temporal punishment due to sins whose guilt has already been forgiven, which the faithful Christian who is duly disposed gains under certain prescribed conditions through the action of the Church" (CCC 1471).

**Indulgence, partial:** an indulgence that removes part of the temporal punishment due to sin (see CCC 1471).

**Indulgence, plenary:** an indulgence that removes all of the temporal punishment due to sin (see CCC 1471).

**Intention:** refers to the minister's intention to do what the Church does in performing a particular sacrament.

**Interdict:** an official prohibition of the Church that excludes a particular person or community from the reception of the sacraments.

**Judgment, divine:** ultimately, all will stand "in the presence of Christ, who is Truth itself, the truth of each man's relationship with God will be laid bare. The Last Judgment will reveal even to its furthest consequences the good each person has done or failed to do during his earthly life" (CCC 1039).

**Justice:** defined as "the moral virtue that consists in the constant and firm will to give their due to God and neighbor" (CCC 1807).

**Justification:** the effect of the grace of the Holy Spirit "to cleanse us from our sins and to communicate to us 'the righteousness of God through faith in Jesus Christ' and through Baptism" (CCC 1987, cf. Rom 3:22). "Justification detaches man from sin which contradicts the love of God, and purifies his heart of sin" (CCC 1990).

**Matter:** in sacramental theology, the essential material component of a sacrament which signifies God's grace; is made effective when joined to the sacramental "form." In the sacrament of penance, the matter of the sacrament is the actual sins confessed by the penitent.

**Mercy:** an expression of God's love and omnipotence "by freely forgiving [our] sins" (CCC 271).

**Merit:** "the recompense owed by a community or a society for the action of one of its members experience either as a beneficial or harmful, deserving reward or punishment." (CCC 2006). "Since the initiative belongs to God in the order of grace, non one can merit the initial grace of forgiveness and justification, at the beginning of conversion. Moved by the Holy Spirit and by charity, we can then merit for ourselves and for others the graces needed for our sanctification, for the increase of grace and charity, and for the attainment of eternal life" (CCC 2010).

**Minister:** in confession, the priest confessor serves as the minister of the sacrament; the minister is "the sacramental bond that ties the liturgical action to what the apostles said and did and, through them, to the words and actions of Christ" (CCC 1120).

**Moral law:** "prescribes for man the ways, the rules of conduct that lead to the promised beatitude; it proscribes the ways of evil which turn him away from God and his love" (CCC 1950)

**Mystery:** the Eastern Christian term for sacrament; see *Sacrament.*

**Occasion of sin**: actions, places, events, or people that may lead us into sin; must be avoided to prevent us from being tempted.

**Pelagianism:** a heresy of the fourth and fifth centuries A.D. that held that one could merit salvation apart from God's grace and the sacraments; essentially, as "salvation by works," i.e., one "earns" heaven.

**Penance:** involves "a radical reorientation of our whole life, a return, a conversion to God with all our heart, an end of sin, a turning away from evil, with repugnance toward the evil actions we have committed" (CCC 1431).

**Penitent:** the recipient of the sacrament of penance (see CCC 1451).

**Predestined:** "God predestines no one to go to hell" (CCC 1036).

**Priesthood, ministerial:** one of the two participations in the one priesthood of Christ (the other participation being the common priesthood of the baptized); it differs essentially from the common priesthood in that the ministerial priest is ordained to minister the sacraments *in persona Christi*; only a priest can validly absolve from sins.

**Punishment:** the just consequences of sin as decreed by God.

**Punishment, temporal:** even after one has been absolved of his or her sins in the sacrament of penance, there may still exist in the penitent "an unhealthy attachment to creatures, which must be purified either herre on earth, or after death in the state called Purgatory" (CCC 1472).

**Punishment, eternal:** the consequence of unrepented grave sin, which "deprives us of communion with God and therefore makes us incapable of eternal life" (CCC 1472). The forgiveness of sin through penance restores man's communion with God, and entails the remission of the eternal punishment of sin.

**Purgatory:** a state after death in which those who die in God's grace remit any remaining temporal punishment due to sin; it is the "final purification of the elect, which is entirely different from the punishment of the damned" (CCC 1031).

**Reconciliation, sacrament of:** another name for the sacrament of penance which emphasizes the effect of restoring the sinner to communion with God and the Church (CCC 1442, 1469)

**Restitution:** see *Satisfaction*.

**Rites:** the "respective liturgical traditions in the communion of the faith and the sacraments of the faith" (CCC 1201); e.g., the Roman rite refers to the liturgical expression of the Diocese of Rome, whereas the Eastern rites include the "Byzantine, Alexandrian or Coptic, Syriac, Armenian, Maronite, and Chaldean rites" (CCC 1203).

**Sacrament:** an efficacious sign of God's grace, "instituted by Christ and entrusted to the Church, by which divine life is dispensed to us."

**Satisfaction:** one must perform acts of satisfaction or restitution "in order to repair the harm (e.g., return stolen goods, restore the reputation of someone slandered, pay compensation for injuries)" caused by sin, both to God and his neighbor (CCC 1459).

**Seal of confession:** the grave obligation by which "every priest who hears confessions is bound under very severe penalties to keep absolute secrecy regarding the sins that his penitents have confessed to him" (CCC 1467).

**Serious sin:** see *Sin, mortal*.

**Sin:** in general, "an offense against God, a rupture of communion with him" (CCC 1440); "an utterance, a deed, or a desire contrary to the eternal law" (CCC 1849).

**Sin of commission:** an offense against the eternal law in "thought, word, or deed" (CCC 1853).

**Sin, mortal:** "sin whose object is grave matter and which is also committed with full knowledge and deliberate consent"

(CCC 1857); involves the loss of sanctifying grace in the soul, which can only be restored by an act of perfect contrition and reception of the sacrament of penance.

**Sin of omission:** a failure to do what one is obligated to do by the divine law (see CCC 1853).

**Sin, venial:** a sin involving "less serious matter" when one "does not observe the standard prescribed by the moral law, or when he disobeys the moral law in a grave matter, but without full knowledge or without complete consent" (CCC 1862).

**Sin, original:** "the original fault freely committed by our first parents," with which "the whole of human history is marked" (CCC 390); remitted in baptism.

**Temptation:** being enticed to consent to committing an action "whose object appears to be good, a 'delight to he eyes' and desirable, when in reality its fruit is death" (CCC 2847).

**Virtues, cardinal:** the four natural virtues are the basis of all other virtues: prudence, justice, fortitude, and temperance (see CCC 1805).

**Virtues, theological:** those virtues that relate directly to God and "dispose Christians to live in a relationship with the Holy Trinity. They have the One and Triune God for their origin, motive, and object" (CCC 1812): they are faith, hope, and charity.

**Tradition, Sacred:** "In order that the full and living Gospel might always be preserved in the Church the apostles left bishops as their successors. They gave them their own position of teaching authority. Indeed, 'the apostolic preaching, which is expressed in a special way in the inspired books, was to be preserved in a continuous line of succession until the end of time.' This living transmission, accomplished in the Holy Spirit, is called Tradition, since it is distinct from Sacred Scripture, though closely connected to it. Through Tradition, 'the Church, in her doctrine, life and worship, perpetuates and transmits to every generation all that she herself is, all that she believes'" (CCC 77–78).

**Unforgivable sin:** the sin of despair, which by its very nature cannot be forgiven insofar as the person who despairs is not willing to accept with faith that he can be forgiven through God's mercy; final impenitence.

**Validity:** For a sacrament to be celebrated validly, the minister must use the proper form (i.e., saying the prescribed words and performing the prescribed actions), and use the prescribed substance (i.e, matter) of the sacrament, e.g., water for baptism, oil for anointing of the sick, bread and wine for the Eucharist, etc.; also, the minister must intend to do what the Church does in the sacrament.

# Index

# About the Authors

**Father Mitch Pacwa, S.J.,** was ordained to the priesthood in 1976. He holds a bachelor of arts degree in philosophy and theology from the University of Detroit, *summa cum laude*, master of divinity and S.T.B. degrees from the Jesuit School of Theology of Loyola University, *magna cum laude*, and a Ph.D. in Old Testament from Vanderbilt University. Father Pacwa has taught at the high school, seminary, and university levels, has lectured at conferences and churches around the world, and has appeared and hosted hundreds of international radio and television programs. His fluency in twelve languages and his extensive travels throughout the Middle East have afforded him a unique understanding of the peoples and cultures of this region. In 2000, he established Ignatius Productions to further promote the Gospel through multi-media teaching presentations.

**Sean Brown** received a master of arts degree in theology and Christian ministry from Franciscan University of Steubenville in 1998. That same year, Sean began graduate studies in film production at the School of Theater, Film, and Television at UCLA. In 2000, he acquired professional certifications in producing and screenwriting. Sean now serves as a theological advisor for the Eternal Word Television Network (EWTN), where he incorporates his background in theology and film to assist in the critical evaluation of video programming content.

# *Indulgenced Prayers*

The following indulgences are granted according to the revised edition of the *Enchiridion of Indulgences* (1999), issued by the Apostolic Penitentiary of the Holy See.

- A plenary indulgence is granted to the faithful who visit the Most Blessed Sacrament in adoration for one half hour under the usual conditions.

- A partial indulgence is granted to the faithful, who recite, according to any legitimate formula, an Act of Faith, Hope, and Love.

## ACT OF FAITH

O my God, who are infallible Truth and can neither deceive nor be deceived, I firmly believe all that you have revealed and propose to my belief through your holy Church, because you have revealed it. I believe that you are one in nature and three in Persons: the Father, the Son, and the Holy Spirit. I believe that you are the Creator of all things and that you reward the just for all eternity in heaven and punish the wicked for all eternity in hell. I believe that Jesus Christ is the Son of God made man, that he suffered and died for my sins and rose from the dead in glory, and that it is only in him through the Holy Spirit that eternal life is given to men. I believe in fine all that your holy Church believes. I thank you for having called me to the true faith, and I protest that with the help of your grace I will live and die in this holy faith.

## ACT OF HOPE

O my God, trusting in your promises and because you are faithful, powerful and merciful, I hope, through the merits of Jesus Christ, for the pardon of my sins, final perseverance and the blessed glory of heaven.

## ACT OF LOVE

O my God, because you are infinite goodness and worthy of infinite love, I love you with my whole heart above all things, and for love of you I love my fellow-men as myself.

⊷

A plenary indulgence is granted to the faithful who recite the *Anima Christi* after reception of Holy Communion and in accordance with the usual conditions.

## ANIMA CHRISTI

Soul of Christ, sanctify me.
Body of Christ, save me.
Blood of Christ, inebriate me.
Water from the side of Christ, wash me.
Passion of Christ, strengthen me.
O good Jesus, hear me.
Within your wounds, hide me.
Separated from you let me never be.
From the malignant enemy, defend me.
At the hour of death, call me.
To come to you, bid me,
That I may praise you in the company
Of your Saints, for all eternity. Amen.